DEATH ON THE RIVER OF DOUBT

DEATH ON THE RIVER OF DOUBT

THEODORE ROOSEVELT'S AMAZON ADVENTURE

SAMANTHA SEIPLE

SCHOLASTIC PRESS/NEW YORK

Library of Congress Cataloging-in-Publication Data available

ISBN 978-0-545-70916-3

10 9 8 7 6 5 4 3 2 1   17 18 19 20 21

Printed in the U.S.A.   23
First edition, January 2017

Book design by Ellen Duda

For Todd

CONTENTS

The Expedition Members

Leaders
Theodore Roosevelt (naturalist)

Cândido Mariano da Silva Rondon (famous explorer)

Officers
João Salustiano Lyra (navigator and cartographer)

José Antonio Cajazeira (medical doctor)

Kermit Roosevelt (sign bearer)

George Cherrie (naturalist)

CAMARADAS (CANOEISTS AND LABORERS)

Paixão Paishon (in charge of the *camaradas*)

Pedrinho Craveiro (camp guard)

Julio de Lima (bowsman)

Simplicio (paddler)

Luiz Correia (steersman)

Antonio Correia (pilot)

Antonio Pareci (paddler)

João (Kermit's surveying assistant)

Henrique (paddler)

Franca (the cook)

Six additional men (*camaradas*)

HUNTING DOGS

Lobo (Rondon's dog)

Trigueiro (Kermit's dog)

PROLOGUE

Knocking on Death's Door

March 27, 1914

Day 29 on the River of Doubt

Time was running out. It was twenty-nine days into the journey, and food supplies were frighteningly low. The men were starving. No one knew how many more miles they would have to travel down the River of Doubt. There was no map to follow, and they had no idea what lay ahead. But Theodore Roosevelt and the men who were with him were certain about one thing. If they didn't hurry and get out of the Amazon jungle soon, they would all be dead.

The winding black river stretched out before them like a slithering snake. Roosevelt sat in his lightly packed canoe, weakened from fever, hunger, exhaustion, and worry. His clothes were damp and sticky, and his eyeglasses were foggy from the thick and steamy air.

A slight breeze offered some relief from the insidious and torturous swarms of biting flies, stinging bees, and disease-spreading mosquitoes. Even with mosquito nets

Map of South America in 1913.

and bug repellent, everyone on the expedition was covered with painful bites.

The dense tropical trees along the river's edge towered overhead, providing shade along the banks, while big-beaked toucans called out with their harsh sounds and flocks of parakeets flashed their green, blue, and red feathers.

Hidden from view, in the dark shadows of the forest, were the Cinta Larga Indians. The silent and stealthy natives kept a close watch on the expedition's every move, with their poison arrows primed and ready to shoot.

While the Cinta Largas watched them from the shadows, the adventurers were looking for monkeys hanging from trees. Sometimes, if they were lucky, they'd be able to shoot one to curb their never-ending hunger pains. But times were tough, and monkeys were a rare indulgence lately.

The expedition had discovered the hard way that in this part of the unexplored Amazon jungle, for some reason unknown to them, food was scarce. The Brazil nuts they had been counting on to sustain them were in short supply, and the piglike tapir, with its prehensile snout, was elusive. And in this section of the river, with the exception of the vicious saw-toothed piranhas, fish were few and far between.

Their progress down the Amazon was slow, and after paddling less than two miles that day, steep hills covered with lush green trees appeared before them. It was a sight to behold. But the beauty was quickly overshadowed by the fearsome sound of rapids just ahead. The adventurers knew all too well that it was dangerous to try to paddle their six canoes through the churning waters, and they couldn't risk losing any more canoes or food.

The men pulled their dugout canoes onto the river's sandy bank and started chopping through the thick vegetation with machetes and knives to make their way around the main rapids. To save precious time, they decided that instead of dragging the heavy canoes over land, they would let them run down the river empty.

The first four empty canoes traveled down to the end of the rapids with great success. The last two, which were tied together, were then set on the course. They rushed down the river but were suddenly turned by the rapids and hurled against some boulders, then became trapped under a tangle of vines and tree branches.

The powerful current pinned the canoes in place, and water quickly rushed into the vessels and sank them. The men knew it was only a matter of time before the force of the water would dislodge the boats, sending them downriver and smashing them to pieces on the edges of jagged boulders.

Everyone quickly ran to help, with Roosevelt being the first to enter the raging river. Using axes, the men chopped away at the rope that tied the two canoes together. Several men made their way to a small island of rocks, just above the canoes, and threw a rope down. Roosevelt and the others below, who were up to their armpits in water and slipping on the mossy rocks, tied the rope to the outermost canoe.

The men above pulled the wet ropes, their hands burning, while those below lifted and shoved, heaving the canoe up. Finally, the canoe was free, and the men slowly dragged it up to safety.

The same procedure was repeated for the second canoe. It was a much-needed victory as both canoes were saved. But the adventurers quickly realized their success had come at a price.

During the ordeal, Roosevelt had slammed his leg into a boulder, gouging his shin. As his blood oozed into the piranha-infested water, he quickly waded to the river's bank and limped back to the campsite at the foot of the rapids.

At first glance, the wound appeared to be minor. But the former president knew what a bloody gash to his leg really meant, especially in the unknown and unforgiving jungle.

Roosevelt was knocking on death's door.

Theodore Roosevelt, 1900.

CHAPTER 1

The Naturalist

Five Months Earlier
October 21, 1913
Rio de Janeiro, Brazil, South America

Since leaving New York two and a half weeks ago, Theodore Roosevelt's steamship, *Vandyck*, had been plagued by bad weather. For the last two days, the voyage hadn't been any different as the steamer inched along the coast of Brazil. Despite this, the passengers onboard—at least the ones who weren't made seasick by the relentless rocking motion— were awed by the sight of huge porpoises and flying fish sailing out of the choppy sea as the vessel cut through the storm.

It was late at night when the city of Rio de Janeiro first came into view, and the ship finally passed the famed Sugar Loaf peak, which marked the entrance into Rio's calm natural harbor. The next morning, on October 21, Theodore Roosevelt and the other passengers woke up and looked out from the deck.

They were greeted on all sides by sparkling blue water, soft sandy beaches, and lush green mountains. Rio's harbor, considered one of the Seven Natural Wonders of the World—like the Grand Canyon—was a breathtaking sight to behold. Even though it was an unseasonably cold morning, there was no doubt that Rio de Janeiro, often called "Marvelous Rio," was a paradise.

At that moment, taking in the view of Rio de Janeiro, Roosevelt had no idea that he was about to receive an offer he couldn't refuse. It was a dangerous offer—one that could easily get him killed. But it was also of great importance. And that was precisely why the danger-loving, thrill-seeking ex-president of the United States wouldn't be able to resist.

Rio de Janeiro, Brazil's capital city at that time, was the second stop on Roosevelt's planned tour of South America. He was there, at the request of the governments of Argentina, Brazil, Uruguay, and Chile, to give a series of lectures on world democracy.

Initially, when Roosevelt received the invitation to come and speak, he turned it down. But a few circumstances led him to reconsider.

First, it would be a chance for Roosevelt to visit his twenty-four-year-old son, Kermit, the third of his six children. For the past two years, Kermit had been working in South America, where he was currently supervising the construction of bridges for the Anglo Brazilian Iron Company.

A few months prior, Kermit had been standing on a steel beam that was being hoisted over the river gorge when the crane slipped. Kermit plunged thirty-five feet, "bouncing like a ball" into a rocky ravine. Lying helplessly on his back, with two broken ribs, a dislocated knee, and two missing teeth, Kermit watched the collapsing bridge come crashing toward him. Amazingly, it just missed killing him.

Although Kermit wrote to his father, "I didn't think I had a chance in a million nor did anyone else," he brushed

Kermit (right) with his brother Archie about a year before Kermit went down the River of Doubt.

off the incident, writing that it was "the chances of the game." Even with Kermit's cool reassurances that he was fine, Roosevelt was worried and wanted to see him. In a letter to his son, Roosevelt wrote:

> *"By George! It was the narrowest squeak I have heard of, and it was a marvel that you got through as well as you did—although two broken ribs, two broken back teeth and water on the knee make an unpleasant aggregate of injuries . . . I cannot say how inexpressibly thankful I am that the accident came out all right. We are all of us much concerned about you."*

Apart from seeing his son, Roosevelt was looking forward to going on a hunting trip through the interior of South America at the end of his speaking tour. He planned to collect new species of birds and other animals for the American Museum of Natural History.

At the time, South America was a very mysterious continent. Large parts were unexplored, leaving a blank space about the size of Montana on the map. The mighty Amazon jungle, which landed squarely in that unknown space, was a dangerous, dense, and nearly impenetrable wilderness.

For those who dared to enter the jungle, many did not make it out alive. Merciless disease, wild beasts, and Indian attacks were a constant threat. Even those who survived its perils warned others against going, calling it suicidal, and telling them to expect nothing less than catastrophe. But that kind of risk didn't discourage Roosevelt—it made him want to go even more.

Though Roosevelt was born into a wealthy family, living a life of privilege and luxury in New York City, he chose to live a "strenuous life," meaning, in his words, "the life of toil and effort, of labor and strife."

As a result, he was a man of action who didn't mind getting his hands dirty—literally. He could often be found baling hay and chopping wood at his country home on Long Island, refusing to let any physical limitations get in his way. But that wasn't always the case.

Roosevelt would grow up to be "as fit as a bull moose," but when he was a child, he was very sickly, frail, and nervous. In fact, his parents didn't expect him to live long.

As a child, Roosevelt suffered from acute asthma, a respiratory disease that caused his airways to constrict, making it difficult for him to breathe. If he was unlucky, an asthma attack could lead to suffocation. At the time, doctors didn't know what caused these attacks, and there wasn't any medicine that could help.

All Roosevelt could do was stay in bed, propped up on pillows, feeling like he was being strangled as he coughed, wheezed, and gasped for breath. Sometimes, in desperation, his father would load him into a horse-drawn carriage and speed through the city streets, hoping the air would be forced into his son's lungs and help him breathe. His parents had him try other remedies of the time—such as smoking cigars and drinking black coffee—but nothing helped.

Since Roosevelt was unwell and often stuck indoors, he spent much of his time reading books. He loved reading about forests and jungles, intensely studying the sketches and detailed information about wildlife—monkeys, vampire bats, lions, cheetahs, and bears, to name a few.

When he was well enough to get out of bed, he carried *The Illustrated Natural History* by J. G. Wood under one arm, and a book about Africa under the other. All his reading about nature sparked a lifelong passion.

Roosevelt, nicknamed "Teedie" by his family, at about seven years old.

One day, when eight-year-old Roosevelt was walking up Broadway in Manhattan, he passed by a market where he was sometimes sent to buy strawberries before breakfast. But on this occasion, something else caught his eye.

"I suddenly saw a dead seal laid out on a slab of wood . . . I asked where it was killed, and was informed in the harbor . . . As long as that seal remained there I haunted the neighborhood of the market day after day," Roosevelt recalled.

Even though Roosevelt didn't have a tape measure, he used a pocket ruler to take the measurements of the seal, a rare find in New York City. He carefully wrote down the measurements in a notebook, just like a naturalist who studies animals and plants. He was eventually given the seal's skull, and he and his cousins displayed it in his bedroom closet, which he called the "Roosevelt Museum of Natural History."

This marked the beginning of Roosevelt's collection of wildlife specimens. Soon the "Roosevelt Museum" displayed tadpoles, bugs, bird nests, and more animal skeletons. Roosevelt's notebook became filled with detailed descriptions of the physical characteristics and habits of the wildlife he observed.

In a short while, the collection of wildlife specimens expanded beyond his closet. He brought home an assortment of live animals, too.

He successfully raised a few baby gray squirrels, feeding them milk through a glass syringe. His tree frog lived in the parlor, while his snapping turtle could be found tied to the laundry tub. In an empty flower pot he housed a sociable family of white-footed mice. But the woodchuck proved to be a mistake. It was a bad-tempered animal, despite Roosevelt's best efforts to tame it.

The only time his mother put her foot down was when dead mice were found stored in the icebox. Roosevelt

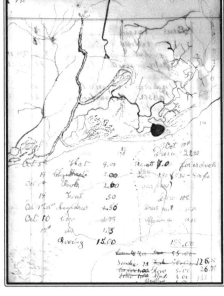

Pages from Roosevelt's field notes of the flora and fauna of New York, New Jersey, and Vermont, plus his hand-drawn map. He began this notebook when he was thirteen years old.

reluctantly got rid of them, feeling it was a terrible "loss to science."

By the age of thirteen, Roosevelt could be found spending many hours during the summer in a cramped and stuffy shop filled with taxidermied animals on the corner of Broadway and Worth Street, not far from where the Brooklyn Bridge was being built. The shop's owner was the tall and white-haired John Graham Bell, who always wore a formal black frock coat.

Bell, who had accompanied the celebrated naturalist John James Audubon on his trip up the Missouri River, was the most famous taxidermist of the time. Roosevelt, who had a growing collection of birds, wanted to learn how to do taxidermy so he could stuff and preserve his specimens himself.

That same summer, Roosevelt also received his first gun, a double-barrel, breech-loading pinfire shotgun. Upon trying to shoot a target, he quickly realized something: He had terrible eyesight.

"It puzzled me to find that my companions seemed to see things to shoot at which I could not see at all," Roosevelt recalled.

The first time Roosevelt put on his new glasses and looked through them, he couldn't believe his eyes.

"[It] literally opened an entirely new world to me." With his newfound sight, the young Roosevelt was ready to take on whatever came next.

CHAPTER 2

A Force of Nature

Thanks to his new glasses, Roosevelt could now identify birds by sight, and not just by hearing them. His bird collection grew even bigger and his observations in his notebook grew longer, especially the following summer when his family took a trip down the Nile River.

"My first real collecting as a student of natural history was done in Egypt on this journey," Roosevelt recalled.

He was determined to become a naturalist and decided that he would study it in college.

But before he went off to college, Roosevelt would undergo another transformation. It began after some boys bullied him when he was thirteen.

Roosevelt wrote, "I made up my mind . . . I would not again be put in such a helpless position; and having become quickly and bitterly conscious that I did not have the natural prowess to hold my own, I decided that I would try to supply its place by training."

So Roosevelt learned to box from a champion fighter. He also lifted weights, rode horses, hiked, ran, swam, rowed, and tried all different types of sports. Although Roosevelt wasn't a natural athlete, he possessed another quality that made him stand out. He was absolutely relentless—always trying and always refusing to give up.

"He's not strong, but he's all grit," his doctor said. "He'll kill himself before he'll even say he's tired."

Along with improvements in his physical and mental strength, the training helped boost Roosevelt's self-confidence. He was no longer riddled with nervousness. Instead, he was fearless.

An older Theodore Roosevelt jumping on horseback,
a hobby that he took up as a teenager.

"There were all kinds of things of which I was afraid at first . . . But by acting as if I was not afraid, I gradually ceased to be afraid," Roosevelt stated.

By 1875, when Roosevelt was seventeen years old, he was no longer a timid and sickly child. He was now bursting with so much energy that he would be called a "steam engine in trousers."

Over the years, Roosevelt's enthusiasm and interest in natural history had not waned. He still planned on studying it at Harvard University.

"When I entered college, I was devoted to out-of-doors natural history, and my ambition was to be a scientific man of the Audubon, or Wilson, or Baird, or Coues type," Roosevelt wrote.

But soon after he started college, he made a surprising decision. He wasn't going to pursue his childhood dream of becoming a naturalist.

"I fully intended to make science my life-work. I did not for the simple reason that . . . They [the college professors] treated biology as purely a science of the laboratory and the microscope . . . I had no more desire or ability to be a microscopist and section-cutter than to be a mathematician. Accordingly, I abandoned all thought of becoming a scientist," he wrote.

By the time he graduated from Harvard with honors and the nickname "Teddy," he surprised everyone again by

A portrait of twenty-seven-year-old Teddy Roosevelt in his buckskin hunting suit.

going into politics. At twenty-three years old, he was elected to the New York State Assembly. Roosevelt quickly established himself as a leader, making newspaper headlines and earning respect for fighting corruption in the state government.

Although his career path had shifted to politics, Roosevelt never abandoned his passion for nature. In fact, he always returned to it whenever he experienced any devastating setbacks.

When Roosevelt was a sophomore in college, his father died of cancer, and he retreated to his family's country home in Oyster Bay, New York. Then he went deep into Maine's wilderness. Roosevelt kept his mind and body in constant motion, trying to fend off his grief and depression. Always carrying his gun, he went on grueling horseback rides and punishing hikes through the woods and fields, keeping a lookout for wildlife specimens to add to his collection.

At the time, Roosevelt wrote about his grief in his diary:

"If I had time to think, I believe I should go crazy . . . Sometimes, when I by accident think of him [his father], it seems utterly impossible to realize that I shall never see him again . . . It is as if part of myself had been taken away . . . When something occurs to bring him vividly before my memory, there come moments of terrible, dull heart pain. He was everything to me: father, companion, friend."

Two years later, on Valentine's Day 1884, twenty-five-year-old Roosevelt was ravaged by grief again when his mother, Martha, died of typhoid fever, a type of bacterial infection. Several hours later, his first wife, Alice, died in his arms from kidney failure, a day after giving birth to their daughter.

"The light has gone out of my life," Roosevelt wrote in his diary on the day they died.

There was only one way Roosevelt knew how to cope with his overwhelming sorrow. He had to take action and do things to stay sane. So even though he was a rising political star as a young state assemblyman, he packed up and moved to the Wild West, where he had bought a ranch. He

Roosevelt (middle) stands between his friends in Medora, North Dakota.

lived the life of a cowboy in the town of Medora, in the Badlands of the Dakota Territory (today's North Dakota). Roosevelt threw himself into the physical demands of cattle roundups, bronco busting, and buffalo and grizzly bear hunting.

At first, the cowboys weren't sure what to make of him. Roosevelt looked different. His eyeglasses triggered distrust because, at that time and in that region, people looked at glasses as some kind of character defect.

Roosevelt also sounded different. He had a high-pitched, cultured voice tinged with a New York accent. Plus, he talked really, really fast. But he proved his mettle.

Even though Roosevelt wasn't a crack shot, the best roper, or the best horseback rider, he had something else that the cowboys valued even more. He wasn't afraid to work hard and was always willing to lend a hand.

"A man of ordinary power, who nevertheless does not shirk things merely because they are disagreeable or irksome, soon earns his place," Roosevelt once stated.

His extreme endurance also impressed the cowboys, especially when he rode hundreds of miles, spending all day and night in the saddle, without complaint.

"That four-eyed maverick has sand in his craw a-plenty," a ranch hand said approvingly.

Although Roosevelt was accepted as a friend, fellow cowboy, and, ultimately, the sheriff's deputy, he never completely severed his ties to New York or politics. He went back to New York frequently to spend time with his family. During his visits, reporters kept tabs on him, printing stories about his cowboy adventures in the newspaper, which kept him in the public eye.

In 1886, the Republican Party urged him to run for mayor of New York, calling him the "Cowboy Candidate." Roosevelt reluctantly accepted the nomination but ended up losing the race.

The following year, Roosevelt hung up his spurs as a rancher. The freezing-cold winter had killed three-quarters of all the cattle that roamed the Badlands, and ranching turned out to be a money-losing venture for him.

But he didn't have any regrets. In fact, looking back on it, Roosevelt believed that he never would have become president of the United States if it hadn't been for his experiences in the Dakota Territory. It helped him further develop his skills as an independent and strong leader.

"It taught a man self-reliance, hardihood, and the value of instant decision," Roosevelt wrote.

Over the years, the work and experience had noticeably transformed Roosevelt's physical appearance.

"What a change!" one newspaper reporter wrote. "Last March he was a pale, slim young man, with a thin, piping voice and a general look of dyspepsia . . . He is now brown as a berry and has increased 30 pounds in weight. The voice . . . is now hearty and strong enough to drive oxen."

One thing that hadn't changed, however, was his heartache, which Roosevelt said was "beyond any healing." Even so, he did find true love again with his childhood sweetheart, Edith Carow, whom he married.

Though Roosevelt went home to New York and eventually returned to a career in politics, he still kept some ties to the West. In fact, when America went to war with Spain in 1898, after the sinking of the U.S. battleship *Maine*, Roosevelt left his job as assistant secretary of the Navy and

Roosevelt (front row, third from the right) with the Rough Riders, who fought in the Spanish-American War.

helped form the 1st U.S. Volunteer Cavalry, also known as the Rough Riders.

Roosevelt, who became a colonel, brought together a group of fierce cowboys, American Indians, Texas Rangers, prospectors, cops, and elite athletes. At forty years old, Roosevelt led them through a hailstorm of bullets as they charged up San Juan Hill, in Cuba, and into a bloody battle. Even when enemy bullets grazed Roosevelt's elbow and another knocked off his glasses, nothing slowed him down. He fought until the Spanish retreated. When Roosevelt returned home, he was not only a hero but also the most famous man in the country.

With his reputation for honesty and his growing popularity, the Republican Party, which was rocked by scandal, nominated Roosevelt for governor of New York. Roosevelt won the election, and soon after, William McKinley tapped him to run as his vice president. But just six months after winning the election, President McKinley was assassinated. Roosevelt, who was only forty-two years old, became the youngest president in the nation's history.

As president, Roosevelt was known as the champion of the working man. He took on big, monopolistic companies, deeming them "hurtful to the general welfare." When Roosevelt brought an antitrust lawsuit against J. P. Morgan, a multimillionaire banker, Morgan was stunned. Morgan thought they were friends, especially since he contributed

President Roosevelt tipping his top hat to the crowd.

large sums of money to Roosevelt's presidential campaign. But Roosevelt treated everyone equally, and that meant calling out people when they were wrong, even if they were his friends.

"I am President of all the people of the United States," Roosevelt said. "Without regard to creed, color, birthplace, occupation, or social conditions. My aim is to do equal and exact justice among them all."

Roosevelt was also known as the guardian of America's land—a cornerstone of his presidency that was influenced by his time spent in the Wild West. He used his power and influence to protect and conserve 230 million acres of American forest, desert, and plains, including the Grand Canyon, Muir Woods, Yosemite, and the Painted Desert, to

The Roosevelt family in 1907.

(Back row, from left to right) Kermit in his riding gear. Alice, Teddy Jr.

(Front row, from left to right) Archie, Theodore, Edith, and Quentin.

name a few. His conservation efforts also saved the buffalo from extinction.

Bringing his unbridled energy and enthusiasm to the job, Roosevelt was a force of nature.

"I have seen two tremendous works of nature in America. One is Niagara Falls and the other is the president of the United States," said John Morley, a British politician, after spending two days with Roosevelt in the White House.

Of all his accomplishments as president, Roosevelt believed that the construction of the Panama Canal was his greatest achievement. The canal was an engineering feat, carving out a fifty-mile-long passage across the Isthmus of Panama that connected the Atlantic and Pacific Oceans. The shortcut shaved off nearly eight thousand miles for ships traveling from New York to California.

Roosevelt was fifty years old when his second term as president ended. He decided not to run again. Instead, he went on a safari in Africa with his son Kermit. The nineteen-year-old loved adventure, just like his dad. Their trip was cosponsored by the Smithsonian Institution. Roosevelt was sent with a team to collect specimens of big-game animals for the Smithsonian's new National Museum of Natural History in Washington, D.C., and the American Museum of Natural History in New York City.

When they returned and the museums received their specimens, Henry Fairfield Osborn, the president of the

American Museum of Natural History and the paleontologist who named the *Tyrannosaurus rex*, said it was "by far the most successful expedition that has ever penetrated Africa."

After his trip to Africa, Roosevelt decided he wanted to run for president in the 1912 election. He didn't think his successor, William Taft, was making good on his promise to finish what Roosevelt started—his program of reform. Roosevelt wanted to get back in office so he could make sure it happened.

Prior to his Brazil expedition, Teddy went on an African safari with his son Kermit, pictured here, and brought back specimens for the National Museum of Natural History and the American Museum of Natural History.

Although Roosevelt was one of the most popular presidents to ever hold office, the Republican Party gave their support to Taft, the current president. So Roosevelt formed the Progressive Party, also known as the Bull Moose Party. This ended up splitting Republican votes between Roosevelt and Taft, which allowed the Democratic hopeful, Woodrow Wilson, to win the election.

When Roosevelt failed to get reelected, he wasn't just disappointed at losing—he was shattered.

"I had expected that we would make a better showing . . . I try not to think of the damage to myself personally," Roosevelt confided to his friend Arthur Hamilton Lee.

So, not long after losing the election, when Roosevelt received the invitation to travel to South America not only to speak but also to spend time in the wilderness, where he could collect new specimens, the former president soon found himself on a steamship heading to Brazil.

His plans were to have a "delightful holiday." He was going to journey through South America in areas that were already on the map. A team of six other American men with varying backgrounds—from natural history to arctic exploration—would accompany him. Roosevelt didn't expect it to be a very dangerous adventure.

That is, until shortly after he arrived in Rio, and his plans changed.

CHAPTER 3

The Offer

October 21, 1913
Rio de Janeiro, Brazil

It was 8:30 a.m., and the sun was bright when Theodore Roosevelt stepped ashore in Rio de Janeiro. He was dressed in a tailcoat and top hat. Walking with his wife, Edith, and son Kermit, Roosevelt was welcomed with military honors. Whistles blew and a band played both the Brazilian and American national anthems. Soldiers, wearing crisp uniforms with shiny buttons and carefully polished shoes, were lined up in neat rows, saluting him.

As the guest of honor, Roosevelt led a parade of important politicians and diplomats down a wide boulevard dotted with palm trees. Walking confidently, with his shoulders thrown back, Roosevelt waved his hand and tipped his top hat to the crowd, revealing a head full of thick brown hair.

The swarms of people, all eager to catch a glimpse of Roosevelt, waved back excitedly. His lively blue-gray eyes were somewhat hidden by the glare of the sun off his wire-rimmed glasses. No one would ever suspect that he was blind in his left eye.

It was a closely guarded secret that Roosevelt had injured his eye during a boxing match while he was president. The people in the crowd only noticed his big, friendly smile, which lit up his face.

Roosevelt's blind eye wasn't the only injury that he kept secret. His left leg was permanently damaged from an accident eleven years before, when a trolley crashed into his horse-drawn carriage. Roosevelt was flung from the carriage and landed on the roadside. His Secret Service agent, who was also thrown from the car, was killed.

Although the public was told that Roosevelt's injuries were minor—a slight bruising—in reality, his left leg was severely bruised. Soon after the accident, a bacterial infection caused his leg to swell up like a balloon from his knee to his ankle. Roosevelt underwent two operations. Refusing any anesthesia, he was fully awake when the surgeon cut open his leg down to the shin bone to drain the abscess.

Despite the surgeon's best attempts, Roosevelt's left leg remained prone to infection at the slightest injury. Since antibiotics hadn't been discovered yet, if another bacterial infection developed, Roosevelt could end up losing his leg. Or even his life.

But Roosevelt's leg hadn't been bothering him lately. In fact, during the journey on board the *Vandyck*, he brought down the house when he danced the sailor's hornpipe—a solo jig where he kicked up his legs and threw out his arms with gusto, imitating the work of a sailor, from rowing a boat to climbing the rigging to saluting his fellow passengers.

Like the passengers on the ship, who cheered on Roosevelt with shouts and applause, the people of Rio greeted him with the same warm enthusiasm at the parade. A newspaper reporter in the crowd wrote that he expected Roosevelt to be much taller than the then-average height of five feet eight inches. Tipping the scale at well over two hundred pounds, he was stout. But at just one week shy of turning fifty-five years old, he still had "the energy of a boy."

After the welcoming ceremony and a tour of the city's recently modernized ports and boulevards, the chauffeured car turned on to Paissandu Street, famous for the lanky royal palm trees that lined each side. At the end of the street, Roosevelt found himself at Palacio Guanabara, or Guanabara Palace, a frosty white and buttery beige neoclassical residence, similar in style to the White House.

Inside, the luxurious palace featured gleaming marble walls, high ceilings, and spacious rooms filled with fancy gold-leaf furnishings. From the dining room window, there was a view of the garden, which was filled with mango trees, palms, exotic flowers, and bubbling fountains. Beyond the garden, down the palm-lined street, was a beautiful view of the bay.

The palace had once been the home of Portugal's Princess Isabel, the daughter of Dom Pedro II, Brazil's last emperor. It was now the home of Brazil's president, Hermes da Fonseca, and it was where Roosevelt would be staying.

After a meeting with President da Fonseca, Roosevelt met with Lauro Müller, the lean and elegant foreign minister of Brazil. Müller was delighted to be meeting with

Palacio Guanabara, the presidential palace in Rio, where Theodore Roosevelt stayed.

Roosevelt. He knew that Roosevelt's expedition through the Brazilian wilderness would garner international attention and raise Brazil's profile in the world.

In a letter to Müller, Roosevelt wrote:

> *"My hope is to make this trip not only an interesting and valuable one from a scientific standpoint, but of real benefit to Brazil, in calling attention to the ease and rapidity with which the vast territory can be traversed, and also to the phenomenal opportunities for development which she [Brazil] offers."*

Roosevelt was also looking forward to the meeting with Müller. He wanted to firm up the details of his plan to go down the well-traveled Paraguay River and the Tapajós River all the way to where it met the Amazon River. But Müller had something else in mind for Roosevelt. It was the chance of a lifetime. An offer that Roosevelt couldn't refuse.

The proposal was for Roosevelt to go deep into an unexplored part of the Amazon jungle in Mato Grosso—Brazil's wild frontier—to map an uncharted river with the renowned explorer Cândido Mariano da Silva Rondon.

A crack shot and expert hunter, Rondon was once described as the "Daniel Boone of Brazil." Born into poverty, he was sent to live on his uncle's ranch in Mato Grosso after his parents died. It was there that Rondon learned how to survive in the untamed wilderness.

At ten years old, he was riding bareback on cattle round-ups with the other cowboys. He spent weeks out on the vast and remote plains, working in the intense heat and rains. Rondon not only helped brand the cattle but also deftly hunted the jaguars that preyed on them, and the wild pigs that destroyed the crops.

When Rondon wasn't working on the ranch, he went to school. He was very smart, especially in mathematics. In 1881, when he was sixteen, Rondon joined the army and earned a scholarship to the Military Academy in Rio de Janeiro, twelve hundred miles away from his home.

At school, he stood out for not only being the best *sertanista*, or frontiersman, but also as a good athlete. At five feet three inches, Rondon wasn't tall, but he was strong and tough. Known for his ferocious energy, he had a seemingly endless supply of endurance. He impressed classmates—one of whom was Lauro Müller—when he climbed Sugar Loaf mountain, scaling it with only a rope.

By 1890, twenty-five-year-old Rondon was a graduate of the Superior War College and an army engineer. It was a combination of his relentless stamina, survival skills, and mathematical mind that made him the perfect candidate to join one of Brazil's boldest and most brutal projects— building the telegraph network.

Cândido Mariano da Silva Rondon.

For over two decades, Rondon, now forty-eight and the commander of Brazil's Telegraphic Commission, explored and mapped the "wild, western wilderness of Brazil." He and his team cut roads, built bridges and telegraph stations, installed telegraph poles, and strung thousands of miles of telegraph lines. It was a superhuman feat that came at a price—the immense suffering of the workers.

Malaria, starvation, Indian attacks, and vicious bites from piranhas, snakes, and insects were all part of the job. For many, it cost them their lives.

Even in the face of constant danger, Rondon maintained a steely resolve. There was still more that he wanted to explore in the Amazon jungle. Four years prior, in 1909, while Rondon was in an unexplored area in Mato Grosso, he discovered the headwaters of an unknown river.

Since no one knew how long the river was, where it would lead, or what they would find, Rondon named it the Rio da Dúvida, or the River of Doubt. At the time of the discovery, Rondon was weak from a bout with malaria and near starvation. He was barely able to hack his way through the jungle, let alone map an unknown river.

When Lauro Müller contacted Rondon, via telegraph, to act as Roosevelt's guide, Rondon balked at the idea at first. He wasn't interested in being anyone's tour guide, not even the former president of the United States. But when it was made clear to Rondon that Roosevelt's intent was scientific in nature, Rondon agreed to do it.

However, the famous explorer didn't think that Roosevelt's current plans, to travel down an already well-known river, "could offer anything new to an Expedition whose object was to unravel unknown aspects of our wilds." So Rondon made a suggestion. He offered to instead take Roosevelt down the unknown River of Doubt to survey it and fill in the blank space on the map.

When Müller presented this offer, Roosevelt listened with rapt attention. He knew that what Rondon was proposing would be a major contribution to science. It was a chance to be a true explorer—mapping an unknown river and discovering new wildlife species in a land never before seen by any naturalist, or any non-native person for that matter. It was an extraordinary opportunity. But it came with a warning.

"Now, we will be delighted to have you do it," said Müller. "But, of course, you must understand, we cannot tell you anything of what will happen, and there may be some surprises not necessarily pleasant."

Roosevelt didn't hesitate.

"Well, by George, that is just what I would like to do," he said to Müller. "To make the try and see what would happen down the river."

When Roosevelt's wife, Edith, heard about the offer, she thought it was a terrible idea—with good reason. Roosevelt's leg wasn't his only health concern.

A year earlier, while Roosevelt was on the campaign trail and getting ready to make a speech, John Schrank, a thirty-six-year-old bartender from New York, shot him at point-blank range in the chest. If it hadn't been for the fifty-page speech tucked in his right breast pocket, along with his spare pair of glasses that were safely stowed in a steel carrying case, the bullet would have pierced his lung.

Despite being shot, Roosevelt gave his fifty-minute speech in a blood-soaked shirt before going to the hospital.

"It takes more than that to kill a Bull Moose!" he said.

The doctors didn't remove the bullet, deeming it unsafe, so it remained lodged in Roosevelt's fourth rib, just an inch away from his right lung.

Regardless of Edith's misgivings, Roosevelt's mind was made up.

He immediately wrote to Henry Fairfield Osborn at the American Museum of Natural History, who was sponsoring the trip, to let him know about the change in plans. Osborn was worried.

"I looked over a route the Colonel [Roosevelt] proposed to follow, and I wrote to him it was so dangerous he could never get back alive . . . This was Colonel Roosevelt's

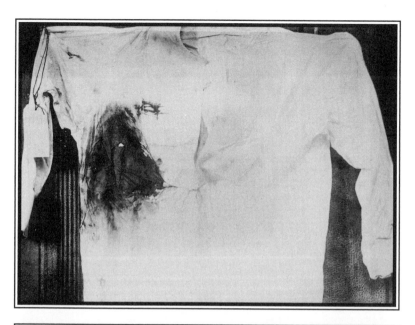

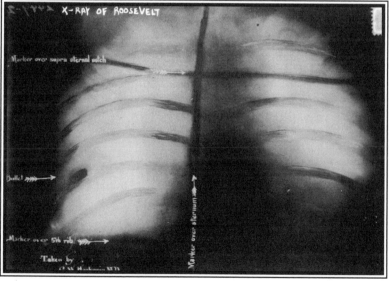

Top: Roosevelt's blood-soaked shirt from the assassination attempt.

Bottom: An X-ray showing the bullet lodged in Roosevelt's chest.

answer: 'I have lived so many lives in my time, and I have had so much more than my share of good things of life that if I have to leave my natural history remains in South America I am willing to do so.'"

Theodore Roosevelt knew that a successful trip down the River of Doubt would be a monumental feat and a valuable contribution to science. And he was determined to be the first to explore the unknown river and change the map of the world. Or die trying.

CHAPTER 4

A Bad Beginning

Four Months Later
February 27, 1914
Day 1 on the River of Doubt

It was the first day on the River of Doubt, and the expedition wasn't off to a good start. Roosevelt thought it must be sometime after twelve o'clock, but he wasn't exactly sure—his watch wasn't working anymore.

It had stopped ticking sometime when he went hunting for a jaguar during the several-hundred-mile journey to reach the River of Doubt. Like the lion in Africa, the jaguar is the king of the South American jungle, and the American Museum of Natural History wanted one for its collection.

Roosevelt was tireless in his hunt for one. When the jaguar swam across alligator-infested lagoons, Roosevelt swam after it, holding his rifle over his head. Even though he gave it his all, the jaguar escaped. And his watch got ruined. Still, Roosevelt had to admit it was an exciting time, so to speak.

But now, while he sat in a heavy wooden dugout made

from a huge, hollowed-out tree trunk on the headwaters of the River of Doubt, Roosevelt was worried. He was supposed to be sitting in a lightweight, state-of-the-art canoe, but that had been abandoned during the punishing journey to get here—along with many of their supplies, including much of their food.

It had taken nearly three months just to reach the River of Doubt. After Roosevelt had completed his two-month speaking tour, he left Asunción, Paraguay, on December 9, 1913, on a gunboat-yacht traveling down the Paraguay River.

Three days later, at the Brazilian border, Rondon's boat came up alongside Roosevelt's yacht, and they met for the first time. Since Rondon didn't speak English, and Roosevelt didn't speak Portuguese—with the exception of *mais canja*, meaning "more chicken soup," his favorite Brazilian dish—they conversed in French. Or, more accurately, Roosevelt *tried* to converse in French. He spoke French very poorly, but that didn't stop him or diminish his enthusiasm. Plus, there was someone he could rely on when his hand-gesturing and broken French stalled the conversation.

Roosevelt's son Kermit, who spoke Portuguese fluently, was also on the expedition—although he didn't want to be there. It wasn't that Kermit didn't love a good adventure. He was just like his father in that respect. It wasn't because he was recovering from a bad case of boils and an attack of malaria—though that didn't help matters. The real problem for Kermit was that he was head over heels in love with his fiancée, and he couldn't wait to get back to civilization so he could marry her.

But his mother had begged her favorite son to go so he could look after his father. Kermit understood why; he was worried, too.

Ever since the trolley accident, when his father's leg was injured, Kermit was very protective of him. Like his father, Kermit wasn't afraid of many things—with the exception of one. He was afraid of his father dying. And if his father's leg got injured again, his death was a real possibility.

So Kermit agreed to accompany him. He wrote a letter to his fiancée, Belle, explaining his decision:

"You see he has never quite recovered from the accident he had when the wagon he was driving in got run over by a trolley. One of his legs is still pretty bad and needs a lot of care."

Kermit also worried that he would regret not going, especially if his father needed him. He explained to Belle:

"If I weren't going I should always feel that when my chance had come to help, I had proved wanting, and all my life I would feel it."

At first, Roosevelt was against the idea of Kermit joining such a dangerous expedition. Plus, he didn't want to interfere with Kermit's wedding plans. In a letter to his daughter-in-law, Eleanor, he wrote:

"I did not like Kermit to come on this trip with me, but he did not wish to be married in my absence, and moreover felt that this semi-exploration business was exactly in his line."

Kermit had insisted, and, truth be told, Roosevelt was happy to have his son with him. Kermit was always a good companion and an excellent outdoorsman, possessing the same relentless endurance as his father. While in Africa together, Roosevelt wrote about Kermit in a letter to his son Archie:

"We worked hard; Kermit of course worked harder, for he is really a first-class walker and runner . . . Kermit has really become not only an excellent hunter but also a responsible and trustworthy man, fit to lead; he managed the whole caravan and after hunting all day he would sit up half the night taking care of the skins. He is also the nicest possible companion."

Throughout his children's lives, Roosevelt had instilled in them his love of nature. He had also entertained them with stories of his hunting adventures in the Dakota Territory and read adventure and nature books to them. One of Kermit's favorite books was *Portraits of the Game and Wild Animals of Southern Africa* by Cornwallis Harris. Like his father, Kermit enjoyed studying the wildlife drawings.

At eight years old, Kermit learned to shoot using the same pinfire shotgun that had been his father's. When Kermit was fourteen, his father sent him to South Dakota, and Deadwood Sheriff Seth Bullock took Kermit camping, fishing, and bear hunting.

Like his father, Kermit was fearless. Ironically, this fearlessness scared his father, and it was a constant source of worry for him, especially when they were hunting lions, elephants, and rhinoceroses in Africa together.

Roosevelt wrote about it in a letter to his daughter Ethel:

"Kermit continues to be a dear, the most pleasant of companions when he is where he can't get into a scrape, and a constant source of worry owing to his being very daring, and without proper judgement as to what he is, and what he is not, able to do. He is very hardy, a very good rider, and bears himself admirably in danger; but he does not know his own limitations, and forgets that at nineteen there is much one has to learn. I am very proud of him, and devotedly attached to him; but Heavens, how glad I shall be to get him out of Africa!"

During the overland journey to reach the River of Doubt, Roosevelt looks on while Kermit (in the white hat) and others examine an animal.

While Kermit and his father shared similar interests and character traits, their personalities were quite different. Kermit was quiet, brooding, and not much of a talker. Where his father had the gift of gab, Kermit had a gift for learning foreign languages. In addition to Portuguese, he also knew Greek, French, and even Swahili, which he learned during their hunting trip to Africa.

So with Kermit as interpreter, Roosevelt and Rondon's first meeting on December 12 officially marked the beginning of the Roosevelt-Rondon Expedition. Transferring onto Rondon's boat, the expedition members traveled down the river, making stops to hunt for wildlife specimens, such as the jaguar, anteater, armadillo, tapir, and an assortment of deer, monkeys, and exotic birds for the American Museum of Natural History.

One month and hundreds of miles later, on January 16, 1914, the expedition arrived at Tapirapuã, the headquarters of the Telegraphic Commission and the last outpost of civilization. The River of Doubt was still nearly four hundred miles away—about the distance from New York City to Pittsburgh, Pennsylvania. Using the telegraph poles and lines as a guide, the men traveled through the barren *chapadão*, or plains, of Mato Grosso, Brazil, on foot, by mule, and, for a short stretch, by automobile in order to eventually reach the start of the river.

To protect himself from the many biting and stinging insects, Roosevelt wore a head net and long gloves so he could write about the expedition at the end of each day.

Roosevelt quickly learned that it wasn't the best time to be traveling through the Brazilian wilderness. It was the rainy season, and everyone and everything was constantly damp and soggy.

"It was not possible to keep the moisture out of our belongings; everything became mouldy [sic] except what became rusty," Roosevelt noted.

Regardless of the weather, the expedition rode mules and marched for over sixteen hours a day, sometimes through sheets of rain and slippery mud, sometimes under the baking sun. And despite the heat and humidity, they were often forced to wear stifling head nets and gloves in order to protect themselves from the clouds of insects that hounded them. The worst were the piums, similar in appearance to a black fly, except the pium bit and sucked their blood. The bite itself didn't hurt, but the itchy welt it left behind caused plenty of discomfort.

"Men unused to the South American wilderness speak with awe of the danger therein from jaguars, crocodiles, and

Two of the animals the Roosevelt-Rondon Expedition may have encountered in the Amazon: left: the jaguar, which is a good swimmer and can also climb trees to ambush its prey; and right: the tapir, which has a flexible snout that can be used as a snorkel when it swims.

poisonous snakes. In reality, the danger from those sources is trivial, much less than the danger of being run down by an automobile at home. But at times the torment of insect plagues can hardly be exaggerated," Roosevelt wrote.

Finally, on February 25, 1914, nearly three months after Rondon and Roosevelt first met, the expedition reached the headwaters of the River of Doubt.

But not everyone had made it. More than half of the pack mules and oxen died from exhaustion and starvation—the loads were too heavy and there wasn't enough grass for them to eat. The expedition was forced to dump supplies to lighten the loads. As a result, the canoes were left behind, along with what remained of the dead animals after the men had eaten what they could.

But most worrisome to Roosevelt was learning that Rondon had left behind food rations for his own men. Rondon thought nothing of it: He and his men would go without their rations to lighten the load. He didn't want Roosevelt and the other Americans to suffer. Rondon's men—including a doctor, a navigator, three soldiers, and thirteen *camaradas* (canoeists and laborers)—were used to going without food and comfort, and their leader figured they could live off the land. Deprivation and hardship were just part of the job of exploring and surviving in the Brazilian wilderness.

Although Roosevelt respected Rondon, he disagreed with him, insisting that the Americans' food rations now be divided evenly among everyone despite the fact that they were already low. Roosevelt believed that every effort should be made to give each person an equal chance of finishing the expedition alive.

Rice, oatmeal, dehydrated potatoes, canned roast beef, gingersnap cookies, sugar, coffee, and chocolate were some of the items packed in watertight tin containers. Each one weighed no more than twenty-seven pounds to ensure that it would float if a canoe capsized.

"We took with us provisions for about fifty days; not full rations, for we hoped in part to live on the country—on fish, game, nuts, palm-tops. Our personal baggage was already well cut down . . . The things that we carried were necessities—food, medicines, bedding, instruments for determining altitude and longitude and latitude—except a few books," Roosevelt wrote.

The canoes and supplies weren't all that were left behind on the overland journey. As every explorer knows, it's crucial to pick the right people for an expedition. Physical strength and mental endurance are essential, but equally important is a willingness to cooperate and work hard for the good of the group. If someone puts his own needs first—whether he is injured, sick, or simply refuses to cooperate—that person becomes the weakest link. If this happens, everyone's chances of survival are threatened.

Roosevelt ended up sending a couple of men from his team home before they reached the river. One was so sick with malaria that he couldn't even start the overland journey. The other complained too much about the physical hardships—demanding that he be allowed to sit in a chair and be carried for the last two hundred miles.

"No man has any business to go on such a trip as ours unless he will refuse to jeopardize the welfare of his associates by any delay caused by weakness or ailment of his," Roosevelt wrote. "It is his duty to go forward, if necessary on all fours, until he drops."

These were the words Roosevelt lived by, and he knew that the expedition would require only the strongest men—and the luckiest.

CHAPTER 5

Survival of the Fittest

February 27, 1914

Day 1 on the River of Doubt (continued)

By the time the expedition reached the headwaters of the River of Doubt, Roosevelt knew who had the best chance of surviving the journey. He chose to bring his son Kermit, and of the six American men that he originally brought with him to South America, he chose only one to continue with them down the River of Doubt. His name was George Cherrie, and he was one of two naturalists that the American Museum of Natural History had hired to accompany Roosevelt.

Tall and lean with salt-and-pepper hair and a handlebar mustache, at first glance forty-eight-year-old Cherrie didn't necessarily look like someone who had spent the last twenty-five years in the South American wilderness. But his trembling hand told another story.

Born and raised in Knoxville, Iowa, Cherrie started out as a mechanical engineer. Yet after only two years behind a desk, the call of the wild beckoned him.

Known as the "prince of tropical American bird collectors," Cherrie had made more than two dozen exploration expeditions in the West Indies and Central and South America, collecting thousands of birds for the British Museum, the Field Museum of Natural History in Chicago, and the American Museum of Natural History, among others. Fluent in Spanish, Portuguese, and French, he had a knack for making friends wherever he went—as well as narrowly avoiding danger and death.

His trembling hand and the big scar on the underside of his arm were the result of a narrow escape from an attack—but not from a wild beast. During his entire career as a naturalist, only one animal had ever unexpectedly attacked Cherrie: a *tamandua*, or lesser anteater.

"Dangers and narrow escapes in the lives of explorers are not always associated with the forces of nature or wild creatures of the forest. Often man becomes the greatest and most deadly menace of them all," Cherrie stated.

For Cherrie, that truth came to light one morning while he was hunting for birds in Peru. Following a trail, he came upon a thicket. After checking the branches to see if there were any birds hiding, he turned and saw a man aiming a double-barreled shotgun at him.

Cherrie recognized him. He had caught the man stealing from him several months before, and the man had

The tamandua, *also known as the lesser anteater,*
can be found in trees and on the ground.

vowed revenge. Without thinking, Cherrie walked toward
him, swung his gun from his shoulder, and pulled the trigger. The man dropped dead.

Then Cherrie noticed a sharp pain in his right arm and
saw blood spurting out. Before the man died, he had managed to shoot off the entire underside of Cherrie's arm,
splintering the bone and severing the tendons.

Dropping his gun, Cherrie grabbed a handkerchief
from his pocket. Using his hand and teeth, he tied a tourniquet around his arm. But it continued to bleed.

Though he was certain he was going to bleed to death,
Cherrie walked back to camp for help. There wasn't much
his companions could do other than tighten the tourniquet.

Roosevelt sits in a canoe ready to begin the journey down the river while Cherrie steps aboard.

The nearest doctor was 150 miles away, which would take three days and three nights to reach. Even though everyone, including Cherrie, thought the wound was fatal, he decided to go.

Since it was too painful bouncing around in a horse saddle, Cherrie walked much of the way. No one would give him anything to eat—with the exception of chicken broth—since it would be a waste of food. Everyone who saw him expected him to be dead by morning. Only he wasn't.

Dazed and in agonizing pain from the infected wound, Cherrie kept pushing himself, walking in his blood-soaked clothes until he caught a boat to the nearest village that had a doctor. Once there, the police wanted to arrest him for murder. But the doctor told them not to bother. Cherrie would be dead by morning. And yet, surprising everyone, he managed to survive.

The police never arrested Cherrie. The man he shot in self-defense was a murderer and thief. Although the big scar and trembling hand were a constant reminder of his narrow escape from death, Cherrie didn't let it bother him. He could still pull the trigger on his gun and was the fastest taxidermist around.

When Roosevelt first met Cherrie, he liked him right away.

"He is one of the best explorers, one of the most nervy men in all dangers, whether they come from the elements, from wild beasts or from wilder men," Roosevelt said.

Along with Roosevelt and Kermit, Cherrie was the only other American on the expedition. Combined with Rondon's team, there were a total of twenty-two people.

As the group trekked to the start of the River of Doubt, they passed by grave sites and the sun-bleached skeletons of oxen and mules from Rondon's previous trips along the road. It was both a reminder and warning that many did not make it out of the jungle alive. When Roosevelt and the others passed the graves marked with wooden crosses, they raised their hats, acknowledging Rondon's workers who had died.

Even more disturbing and unsettling were the graves of Rondon's soldiers who had been attacked by the Nhambiquara Indians. After killing the men with their six-foot-long arrows—the tips of which were poisoned with a plant extract called curare—the Nhambiquara buried them in an upright position, with their heads and shoulders sticking out of the ground.

Like the United States, Brazil had a population of different Indian tribes native to the land. From the time the first Portuguese explorer, Pedro Álvares Cabral, discovered Brazil in the year 1500, the Indian population was negatively impacted—from disease to enslavement to encroachment on their land and way of life.

Cut off from civilization, the Nhambiquara Indians were adept at hiding from plain view in the rain forest. So much so that some people believed that the Nhambiquara were essentially a myth. At least they had until 1907, when Rondon and his men were shot at. The first arrow whizzed by Rondon's face, and he mistook it for a bird. But the second arrow grazed his hat. And the third hit him in the chest. By chance, Rondon escaped injury. The thick leather rifle strap he was wearing stopped the poisoned arrow from tearing into him.

With the arrow still sticking out of his strap, Rondon fired his rifle into the air, scaring the Indians off. At first, Rondon was outraged. He and his men wanted to kill them, to gain the upper hand.

A Nhambiquara Indian with his bow and arrow.

"Why I never dreamed that such a treasonous attack could happen . . . I escaped a shameful death at the hands of traitors!" Rondon wrote in his diary.

By the following day, however, he'd had time to collect both the Nhambiquara arrows and his thoughts. Rondon, who was part Terena and Bororo Indian as well as Portuguese, decided against a counterattack.

Rondon realized that from the Indians' perspective, he was invading their homeland. He understood that they were protecting their territory, just like he was trained to do in the military.

"Attacking us, they were doing no more than defending their own lives and those of their women and children . . . The most overwhelmingly important thing to avoid is adding fuel to the flame . . . We must do everything possible to show them . . . that we have no other intention than of protecting them," Rondon wrote.

Drawing from his experience in establishing peace with the nearby Pareci Indians, Rondon knew the best approach was to gain the Nhambiquara Indians' trust. To do this, he and his men needed to remain passive and peaceful—no matter what. He ordered his men to never fight back even if they were under attack—even if it killed them, literally. His motto was "to die if necessary; to kill never."

Rondon was so passionate about protecting the native people of Brazil that in 1910 he helped set up the Indian

Protection Service. His ambition was to protect the South American Indians and preserve their culture, striving for a peaceful coexistence. He was the liaison between the South American Indians and the Brazilian government.

But the Nhambiquara, cut off from society in the rain forest, weren't aware of Rondon's decision. Although the explorers retreated, the Nhambiquara stealthily followed them. They terrorized Rondon and his men, attacking them at night when the men were sleeping in their hammocks, and stealing their food and killing their pack animals.

In order to break through the communication barrier and begin peace negotiations with the Nhambiquara, Rondon set up a phonograph and played records. Like the Pied Piper, the music lured the Indians out of their hiding places and into Rondon's campsite. Once there, Rondon gave them a generous peace offering—gifts of food, beads, handkerchiefs, and metal tools such as knives and axes.

The Nhambiquara were nomadic hunters and gatherers with Stone Age tools. Rondon's gifts of metal tools were a persuasive means of communication, allowing him to forge a fragile friendship.

Still, things weren't always friendly. Whenever the Indians visited Rondon's camp, something was usually missing after they left. And if the Nhambiquara ever felt threatened or betrayed, they settled the matter by killing the person.

Although Roosevelt respected Rondon and his mission, he wasn't going to die for the cause. Roosevelt viewed the Nhambiquara as "light-hearted robbers and murderers."

"He is on remarkably good terms with them, and they are very fond of him—although this does not prevent them from now and then yielding to temptation, even at his expense, and stealing a dog or something else that strikes them as offering an irresistible attraction," Roosevelt wrote.

It was anybody's guess if the Indians might attack them on the expedition. And since the River of Doubt was previously unexplored, it was possible that other tribes lived there that no one knew about.

"Anything might happen," Roosevelt wrote. "We were about to go into the unknown, and no one could say what it held."

Pushing off from the shore, the *camaradas* paddled the dugouts, sliding through the smooth, dark water and moving briskly toward the shadowy forest in the horizon. The river ran deep and wide from all the rain, covering up rocks and fallen trees. As the journey into the unknown began, no one could have suspected that there would soon be a criminal among them.

From the wooden bridge, Roosevelt heard someone shout, "Good luck!"

He would need it.

The last of the seven canoes begins the journey down the River of Doubt.

CHAPTER 6

Into the Unknown

March 1, 1914

Day 3 on the River of Doubt

Before the sun had a chance to rise, and the forest was still eerily quiet, Roosevelt emerged from his tent. It was pitched on flat ground near the river's edge.

Wearing only his birthday suit, Roosevelt waded into the cold black water. He knew it was a risk swimming with hungry piranhas.

Adding to the risk was the fact that no one knew how to prevent an attack or what to do if the piranhas did strike. Some people advised against splashing in the water, while others, like Cherrie, swore that splashing was the only way to keep them away. But one thing was certain: Even the smallest drop of blood attracted the piranhas like a nail to a magnet.

"They are the most ferocious fish in the world," Roosevelt wrote. "Even the most formidable fish, the sharks or the barracudas, usually attack things smaller than themselves. But the piranhas habitually attack things much larger than themselves. They will snap a finger off a hand incautiously trailed in the water . . . they will rend or devour alive any wounded man or beast; for blood in the water excites them to madness."

Even so, that didn't stop anyone from getting into the water. Not even Rondon, who was missing a little toe after a piranha bit it off. Or Cherrie, who had scars on his shoulder and body from a piranha attack.

Cherrie remembered the day he was attacked after slipping from a tree limb and slicing his arm open in the fall:

"I realized that I was bleeding and that my blood would instantly incite an attack by the murderous fish . . . the

A bloodthirsty piranha.

lightning-like rapidity of the piranha left me little chance to escape unhurt . . . But I retained enough of my reason to know that my one chance of escape lay in keeping the fish at bay before they became crazed with the taste of blood. So not only did I strike out for the shore but I set up a violent motion of twisting and rolling and splashing with my arms and legs. Even then I felt a blow and a sharp pain in my shoulder that told me one of the fish had struck. All I could do was to continue my furious splashing. Luckily I succeeded in reaching the shore, though badly bitten . . . I know that had I been even slightly stunned by my fall I should never have lived to tell the tale."

After bathing in the river and eating breakfast, the men of the Roosevelt-Rondon Expedition lined up and stood at attention. Rondon, dressed in his military uniform and with his faithful dog, Lobo, by his side, read aloud his Order of the Day, which included their work assignments and goals. He would also always nail a sign to a wooden post that was carved with the letters *R-R* (for Roosevelt-Rondon), the camp number, the date, and how far they'd traveled down the River of Doubt.

Unfortunately, they hadn't made much progress. Traveling at a slothlike pace, it had taken three days to map eight miles.

"The course is extremely tortuous . . . twisting and turning in every direction. The boatmen have some strenuous times in getting the boat around some of the curves," Cherrie wrote in his diary.

The surveying group, which was responsible for plotting the course and measuring the length of the river, had their work cut out for them. Even though they were the first to leave each morning, they were the last to arrive at the new camp.

Kermit, who was in the lead canoe with his hunting dog, Trigueiro, was in charge of "sighting." He looked for an area along the shoreline that gave an unobstructed view up and down the river, which was usually at one of the many twists and turns.

The *camaradas* in his canoe, Simplicio and Henrique, paddled and steered the small canoe to the shoreline. Kermit then hopped out of the canoe—never certain if he was going to be greeted with a poison arrow shot by a hidden Indian.

After using his machete to hack his way through the dense foliage—all while getting stung and bitten by wasps and ants—Kermit would set up the sighting rod. The rod had two disks attached to it, one white and one red, which were 1 meter apart.

When the sighting rod was set up, Rondon's loyal right-hand man, Lieutenant João Salustiano Lyra, used a telemeter, an instrument that measured the distance from his canoe to the sighting rod. At the same time, Rondon used a compass to note the direction of the river. Later, Lyra, who was a cartographer, would plot the course and calculate the distance.

This "fixed-station" survey method was an accurate way to map the river, but it was time-consuming. On the first afternoon, Kermit planted the sighting rod 114 times, taking five hours to map six miles.

"Lots of ants; rather hard work," he wrote in his diary.

The slow speed worried Roosevelt. Unlike Rondon, he believed a detailed map wasn't necessary. Given their low food supplies, traveling down the river in a timely and efficient manner was crucial to their survival.

"We did not know whether we had one hundred or eight hundred kilometers to go, whether the stream would be fairly smooth or whether we would encounter waterfalls or rapids . . . [or] meet hostile Indians . . . We had no idea how much time the trip would take. We had entered a land of unknown possibilities," Roosevelt wrote.

It was also becoming apparent that the possibility of supplementing their food rations with game, such as the tapir, looked bleak. With the exception of a school of otters swimming in the river, the surrounding area so far had not been full of wildlife. The high waters along the shoreline had caused some of the animals to migrate inland, deep into the Amazonian rain forest.

Roosevelt was keeping a close eye on everything, but he wanted to be "more than courteous and polite and friendly with my Brazilian companions." So, for now, he decided it was best not to say anything. Besides, for all he or anyone else knew, the river might get easier to navigate as they went along.

Not long after Rondon read his Order of the Day, the surveying team took off down the river to begin their long day's work.

It was about eleven o'clock in the morning when Roosevelt, Cherrie, and José Antonio Cajazeira—the expedition's "cool and plucky" medical doctor—climbed into the canoe they shared. It was the largest and most difficult one to maneuver.

"We had seven canoes, all of them dugouts. One was small, one was cranky, and two were old, waterlogged, and leaky," Roosevelt noted.

There were also three *camaradas* in Roosevelt's canoe. Luiz Correia was the steersman, Julio de Lima was the bowsman, and Antonio Pareci was the paddler.

"They were expert rivermen and men of the forest, skilled veterans in wilderness work. They were lithe as panthers and brawny as bears. They swam like waterdogs. They were equally at home with pole and paddle, with axe and machete . . . They looked like pirates," Roosevelt wrote.

One of the biggest and strongest *camaradas* was Julio de Lima. When Rondon first hired him to go on the expedition, Julio was enthusiastic. This was unusual, since many men viewed working for Rondon as a form of punishment. It wasn't just the harsh and isolated wilderness that deterred them. Rondon was a strict disciplinarian, ruling his men with an iron fist.

His tough and authoritarian leadership style was necessary in the wild where disease, Indian attacks, and the inhospitable environment relentlessly threatened everyone's lives. Rondon couldn't risk a mutiny.

Expedition members João Salustiano Lyra (left) and Dr. José Antonio Cajazeira (right).

If any of his men showed insubordination, Rondon was quick to put them in their place. In the past, this had included brute force, such as beating them with a switch (which he later regretted). In any case, with his reputation as a no-nonsense leader as well as the grueling work, Rondon had to pay his men six to seven times more than the going rate for hired workers.

In comparison, Roosevelt's leadership style was much more approachable. Even though he couldn't speak Portuguese, the former president's gregarious nature broke through the language barrier. One way he showed his appreciation to the *camaradas* for their backbreaking work was to share a chocolate bar from his provisions. He did this every day at noon.

"It was a strange form of food for the Brazilian interior, and was especially enjoyed by the laborers," said Rondon. "Those little daily acts of thoughtfulness were much appreciated and the men soon loved him."

Cherrie described Roosevelt as "the ideal camp mate."

"We all felt the honesty of the man and his unselfish attitude," he said. "[Roosevelt] was a good fellow to have in any camp party. He always wanted to do his share of the work and was the soul of good spirits and comradeship."

Cherrie and the others especially enjoyed Roosevelt's ability to tell a good story, keeping everyone entertained with tales of his adventures in the Wild West, in Africa, and as president.

"He was a charming companion . . . He was what we Brazilians call a *'pandego'* . . . 'the life of the party,'" said Rondon. "And talk! I never saw a man who talked so much. He would talk all the time he was in swimming [sic], all of the time during meals, traveling in the canoe and at night around the camp fire. He talked endlessly and on all conceivable subjects."

Roosevelt wasn't just a good talker with a sharp memory. He was also a good listener with a genuine curiosity about others.

"His interest was so whole-hearted and obvious that the shyest, most tongue-tied adventurer found himself speaking with entire freedom," Kermit wrote. "Every one with whom we came in contact fell under the charm. Father invariably thought the best of a person, and for that very reason every one was at his best with him—and felt bound to justify his confidence and judgment."

But there was always the exception. And, as Roosevelt would soon witness, when a situation becomes so desperate and dangerous that death seems inevitable, fear can bring out the worst in people.

It was only a matter of time.

CHAPTER 7

The Roar

March 2, 1914
Day 4

March 2 started out as a delightful day. There had hardly been a drop of rain, and the river was calm. The canoes traveled steadily, zigzagging along the bends in the river. The men knew the direction they were heading—due north—but the river and the surrounding rain forest could still hold plenty of surprises.

"As usual, it was very beautiful," Roosevelt wrote. "And we never could tell what might appear around any curve."

Sometimes the river took them through the swampy forest, where the water gently flowed for miles through the trees. Yesterday, they had suddenly stumbled upon an Indian village, passing palm-leaf shelters along the shore and some sticks poking out of the water, which was all that was left of the Indians' fishing trap. The river then whisked the canoes under some braided vines that reached across the banks. The vines were remnants of a handrail from a footbridge that the rising waters had washed away.

These were the first signs the expedition had found that indicated humans lived along the River of Doubt. Fortunately, this Indian village was abandoned. Otherwise, their arrival may have resulted in a surprise attack.

Rondon wasn't sure, but he thought it might be the Navaitê Indians, who had once lived there. They were a subtribe of the Nhambiquara Indians.

Why they had abandoned the primitive village was anyone's guess. The rising river could have forced them inland, or disease may have wiped them out, or another Indian tribe could have attacked and killed them all. And there was also the possibility that the Indians were still nearby, hiding and watching every move the men made.

The expedition didn't linger near the village long. With the aid of the *camaradas'* poles and paddles, they continued down the river.

During the long hours in the canoe, Roosevelt and Cherrie kept a lookout for wildlife. So far their collecting had been a success. From the moment Cherrie first set foot in Brazil, he had already added one thousand birds to the museum collection. They had also collected 250 mammals, which included the prized jaguar. Those specimens had been sent back to the American Museum of Natural History in New York before they started their river journey.

Animals of the rain forest: left: The slow-moving sloth hangs out in the canopy; right: Is it a branch or a bug? The walking stick insect is great at camouflage.

Although Cherrie usually went hunting each morning and had added about a dozen more birds to the collection, he and Roosevelt didn't see much wildlife as they canoed down the river. While the rain forest had more kinds of animals than any other habitat—with many species still undiscovered—they were often difficult to see.

Some, such as jaguars and tapirs, had migrated to higher ground during the rainy season, but there were still many animals all around them. Roosevelt and the others couldn't see them because the animals were hiding and blending in among the densely packed leaves that make up the upper level of the towering trees, known as the canopy. Some animals, like the sloth, rarely come down from the canopy to the ground. Others, like monkeys, alternate between the ground and the trees.

But even when the animals are in plain view, many have protective coloration, which acts as camouflage. This prevents predators from seeing and eating them. Sometimes what appears to be a leaf or stick in the rain forest is really an insect, fooling a would-be predator by blending in with its surroundings.

Nevertheless, there were times when Roosevelt and Cherrie were lucky. Yesterday, for instance, after passing the abandoned Indian village, they had heard a noise coming from the trees above. It sounded like "eeolk, eeolk."

Cherrie looked up and caught sight of a dark gray monkey with a potbelly and prehensile tail. It was a woolly monkey, also known as a barrigudo. He aimed his gun at it and fired. The bullet met its target.

Afterward, Cherrie skinned the monkey and handed it over to Franca, the cook, who prepared it for dinner that night. It was the first time Roosevelt had tasted monkey meat, and he wrote that it was "very good eating."

The monkey stew was particularly tasty to Roosevelt because he knew he was lucky to be alive. Before he had sat down to dinner last night, he was almost killed.

It happened when the *camaradas* hurriedly set out to

clear the area for their campsite, cutting away the thick vegetation and brushing aside the dead leaves. No one noticed the poisonous coral snake—until a *camarada*'s bare foot almost stepped on it.

Frightened, the *camarada* swung at it with his ax, trying to kill it. But he missed, and the three-foot snake shot forward, heading toward Roosevelt.

Roosevelt quickly lifted his foot and stomped down on it. Then he lifted his other foot and stomped again, trying to crush the snake's head. But Roosevelt missed, and the snake opened its mouth, bared its venomous fangs, and bit down hard on his boot.

The poisonous coral snake is bright yellow and red.

Roosevelt knew that this was bad—very bad. A bite from a coral snake can lead to paralysis and death.

"But I had on stout shoes," Roosevelt noted. "And the fangs of these serpents—unlike those of the pit-vipers—are too short to penetrate good leather."

It was a surprising stroke of good luck.

The fact that Roosevelt had lived another day, and was now sitting in a canoe with his fang-bitten boot looking for wildlife, proved it. But, as his canoe glided along another curve in the river, Roosevelt wasn't feeling so lucky.

It was midafternoon when he and the men noticed that the current was starting to pick up its pace. The water flowed faster and faster, and soon it was running at a furious speed.

Suddenly, the canoes were flying down the river, bouncing and bumping over very rough water, and in the distance the sound of a roar grew louder and more thunderous.

The roar was a warning, and the men hurriedly paddled their canoes toward the shore for safety. The expedition knew that they were facing one of their most dangerous and deadly foes of all: rapids.

With one glance, they knew it would be impossible to paddle the canoes down the river. Foaming white water rushed violently over smashed rocks that were thrown on top of one another.

If they were reckless and tried to run the rapids, their

wooden canoes would most likely capsize and get ripped to pieces. If the men didn't drown in the rapids, those who survived would be left stranded in the jungle without food, weapons, tools, and shelter.

With no choice but to stop, the *camaradas* began setting up camp. Meanwhile, Rondon and the rest of the men cut through the undergrowth along the river's edge to determine how far the rapids went.

For nearly a mile, the rapids swept on, interspersed along the way with a number of waterfalls.

"But the extraordinary thing," Cherrie wrote in his diary, "is that just at the foot of the rapids proper the stream rushes into a narrow gorge with almost perpendicular walls of rock. In one place it is barely five feet across!"

How deep the water at the narrowest point went could only be guessed at, but Cherrie was able to stand on one side of the river's bank and touch the other side with the muzzle of his rifle.

Their progress down the river was at a standstill. In the four days since starting their journey into the unknown, the expedition had traveled only twenty miles down the river. They knew that their sole choice now was to build a portage, or overland route, so they could drag their canoes to the point where the rapids ended. This was not an easy undertaking, and it would take days to build the trail.

Using machetes and axes, they cut through the jungle's

dense foliage. They also chopped down trees and lined them up, side by side, along the newly cut path. The tree trunks acted as rollers, allowing a man to harness the canoe to his body with a rope and pull—like a horse pulling a wagon—while another man stood behind it with a pole and pushed and prodded the canoe as it moved sluggishly over the makeshift "road."

The precious time and hard physical labor needed to carry all their supplies and transport the canoes over dry land wasn't their only problem. When Rondon scouted the area across the river, he found what was left of another abandoned Indian village.

Even more troubling was something Kermit found while walking near the campsite—two freshly cut branches, laid carefully side by side, in plain view. Each small branch had eight leaves.

The men recognized it as a message from the Indians. This type of signal was a common form of communication in the wild. What it meant, they didn't know. But it was clear that they weren't alone. After that, no one left the camp without his rifle.

CHAPTER 8

Welcome to the Jungle

March 4, 1914

Day 6

Two days later, Roosevelt and Cherrie woke up not a second too soon to find their tent crawling with thousands of termites. The insects were eating everything in their path, including Cherrie's rain poncho, mosquito netting, and duffel bag.

"My poncho that I had spread on the ground beneath my hammock was literally alive with them," Cherrie wrote in his diary.

When Roosevelt leaned over the side of his cot and looked at the floor, he saw moving patches of red and green. Recognizing that the termites were eating his wide-brimmed sun helmet, he reached down and grabbed it. Brushing and shaking off the termites, he held up and inspected what remained of a spare pair of underwear. Cherrie and Kermit burst into laughter. This time, Roosevelt didn't find it very funny.

"My socks had totally disappeared and so had most of my underclothing," Roosevelt said. "And I badly needed that change that very day."

From the time they set up camp to stop and build the portage, the bugs were worse than ever. Everyone was suffering from insect bites.

"The little bees were in such swarms as to be a nuisance. Many small stinging bees were with them, which stung badly," Roosevelt wrote. "We were bitten by huge horse-flies the size of bumblebees . . . The boroshudas were the worst pests; they brought the blood at once, and left marks that lasted for weeks."

Despite wearing head nets and using the newly invented "fly dope," now known as insect repellent, there was no way to truly get rid of the bugs. The effectiveness of the fly dope ointment wore off after about a half hour—partly because they were sweating profusely from the intense heat. Even so, they were glad to have the repellent, especially at night, when they were trying to sleep.

"We have suffered more . . . than any previous day with insects," Cherrie wrote in his diary. "My hands, and ears especially, itch and burn almost intolerably."

The shoeless *camaradas* were dealing with painfully swollen bare feet. And Julio, the biggest and strongest *camarada*, was quickly losing his initial enthusiasm for his job. However, even amid the nearly constant biting and stinging

After cutting and clearing a path by hand, the men dragged the canoes over the portage, made up of the log rollers that they had chopped down in the rain forest.

insects, the men made headway with the portage, finishing it in two days.

They then began the grueling task of lugging the seven empty canoes out of the river and up the steep riverbank to the portage. Kermit, who was not only suffering from insect bites but also from another outbreak of boils, still managed to help. Together, he and Rondon's right-hand man, Lyra, pulled and pushed the biggest and heaviest canoe.

By the following day, on March 5, at noon, the canoes were finally back in the river, loaded down with their cargo and ready to go. When Roosevelt climbed into his canoe, looking it over, he could see that all their hard work had come at a price.

"It not only cost two and a half days of severe and incessant labor, but it cost something in the damage to the canoes," Roosevelt stated. "One in particular, the one in which I had been journeying, was split in a manner which caused us serious uneasiness as to how long, even after being patched, it would last."

With swollen hands, faces, and feet, the men finally continued on down the river. They found some slight relief from the biting insects—as long as the canoes were in constant motion. But when they spotted a huge "bee-tree" along the bank, they didn't hesitate to stop.

The *camaradas* took their knives and axes and gouged holes in the tree. A thick milky liquid oozed out, which they eagerly drank. Roosevelt wasn't sure he liked it.

But when Luiz, the steersman in Roosevelt's canoe, took his ax and chopped into the hollow of the tree, Roosevelt could see a waxy formation. Inside was the hive where the stingless bees stored their honey. Everyone greedily ate some.

"The honey was delicious, sweet and yet with a tart flavor," Roosevelt wrote.

Before leaving, some greenish-black, white, and brown feathers caught Kermit's attention. It was the turkey-like guan. He quickly grabbed his rifle and fired, expertly hitting his target. Tonight, the cook, Franca, would make *canja*—Roosevelt's favorite stew. But it wouldn't be nearly enough to curb the hunger pains of the twenty-two men.

Back in their canoes, Rondon, Kermit, and Lyra continued to survey and map the winding river. Overall, it was slow going. Roosevelt still worried about the time involved in making a detailed map—not to mention the time lost in building the portage.

Since the start of the journey, they had zigzagged down the curvy river, traveling about sixty miles, which averaged to seven and a half miles a day so far. But if they drew the distance as a straight line on the map, the number of miles they had traveled was much shorter—by about half. And no one knew how many more miles the river ran.

"What is ahead is absolutely unknown . . . for we had no idea where we would come out, how we would get out, or when we would get out," Roosevelt wrote.

Roosevelt (left) and Rondon stand on a tall rock formation to get a better view of the rapids.

At three o'clock that afternoon, the current suddenly picked up its pace, and the men again heard the ominous roar of rapids. The *camaradas* quickly paddled the canoes to the bank.

They soon found a narrow path alongside the river. The path had been beaten down by the four- and three-toed feet of the piglike tapirs that usually live near the water because they love to swim. Following the trail, the men scouted the area.

The rapids stretched on for a mile and included two waterfalls. Although the men didn't want to, they knew that they had to stop and build another portage. Running the rapids was too risky, as Roosevelt noted:

"It would be silly to make the attempt on an exploring expedition, where the loss of a canoe or of its contents means disaster . . . Our canoes would not have lived half a minute in the wild river."

Four grueling days later, the canoes were back on the river. But the expedition traveled only one mile before reaching another set of impassable rapids. Disheartened, the men moored their canoes securely to some trees and set up camp.

That night the rain fell hard, and while they slept, no one had any idea that the river was quickly and steadily rising.

CHAPTER 9

Misfortune

March 11, 1914
Day 13

It was still raining the next morning when the men woke up and discovered that two canoes were missing. They hurriedly untied one of the remaining canoes and set off, frantically searching the river for their lost canoes. But all they found were pieces of wood, the last remaining fragments of their smashed canoes.

Roosevelt figured that the rising river caused the leaky canoe to sink, pulling the canoe it was tied to under as well. Once the canoes were sunk, the water yanked and pulled them free from their moors. The canoes were then swept away, crashing into rocks that pulverized them to bits.

It was a disastrous setback. There wasn't enough room for all the men and cargo in the five remaining canoes. Their only option was to build another canoe, but it would take days.

Cherrie expressed his worry in his diary:

"This morning our first serious misfortune faces us! The two old big canoes . . . broke away last night and are smashed on the rocks! There is nothing for us to do but stop and build one or two new canoes. This means time and the eating into our limited supply of provisions!"

The men immediately set out looking for a suitable tree to build a canoe. It continued to rain heavily, but they eventually found a huge tatajuba, a type of rubber tree, that was five feet in diameter around the base. Under Rondon's watchful eye, the *camaradas* got busy and chopped it down. By evening, they began the time-consuming task of hollowing out and shaping the hard yellowish wood into a canoe.

For the next few days, the *camaradas* worked all day in shifts, not stopping until near midnight. Rondon never left their side while they worked. He wanted to make sure that the *camaradas* never let up.

Camarada Paixão Paishon, who had proved his mettle working in the wilderness for Rondon's Telegraph Commission, labored so hard that his trousers were shredded. The rest of the *camaradas* worked tirelessly, too—except for one—the strongest one of all, Julio. Roosevelt described Julio as an "utterly worthless . . . lazy shirk."

Rondon agreed. "When we were able to discover his bad qualities . . . we were so far advanced in the river that it was impossible for us to rid ourselves of his presence, and we

Building a new canoe was backbreaking, tedious work that cost the expedition precious time.

therefore had to resign ourselves to keeping him with us until the end of the journey."

There was no doubt that morale was low.

"There isn't anyone of our party that will not be very thankful when this trip draws to a close. There are too many uncertainties and possibilities to face to make it a thing to anticipate with gusto," Cherrie wrote in his diary.

While Rondon tried to keep the *camaradas* motivated to build a new canoe, Roosevelt and Kermit went into the forest to hunt for food. Walking among the giant trees with their snakelike lianas, or vines, hanging down, Roosevelt noted the stillness and silence in the forest.

Hours later, despite Roosevelt's best efforts, he came back empty-handed. Luckily, Kermit returned with the chicken-like curassow for a pot of *canja*. They had also started to eat the celery-like palm tops. But the men were slowly starving.

Roosevelt and Cherrie had taken the time to sort and count their food rations. If it turned out that the River of Doubt was a tributary of the Amazon River, they estimated that they had to travel another four hundred miles. Based on their current average speed and the number of miles that they had already traveled, they would run out of food thirty-five days before they would finish their journey.

"There may be very serious times ahead of us," Cherrie wrote.

The curassow, which looks somewhat similar to a chicken, whistles when it senses danger and prefers to run instead of fly.

Along with the lack of food, illness had started creeping up on them. One of the *camaradas* was suffering from malaria. And Roosevelt wasn't feeling well, either.

Malaria was the most feared and the most prevalent disease in the Amazon. This potentially fatal illness is caused by a parasite that is spread by the female *Anopheles* mosquito.

The first signs of malaria include a teeth-chattering chill along with a pounding headache, followed by a dangerously high fever, and then profuse sweating. At this point, the victim is usually extremely exhausted and weak, and can do nothing but sleep.

This is followed by vomiting, diarrhea, convulsions, and in some cases if left untreated, kidney failure, seizures, confusion, and death.

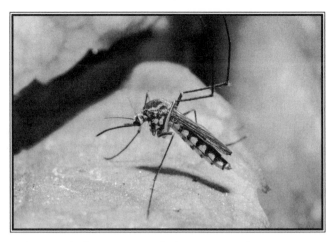

The Anopheles *mosquito, which transmits malaria parasites.*

At the time, the only medicine to combat malaria was quinine, which is extracted from the bark of the cinchona tree. For the Roosevelt-Rondon Expedition, Dr. Cajazeira had luckily brought plenty of it.

Although Roosevelt was showing signs of malaria, he wasn't going to let it prevent him from doing whatever he could to help.

On March 14, four days after the two canoes were destroyed, the group woke up to more heavy rain. Despite the stormy weather, the *camaradas* finished building the new canoe by noontime. About an hour later, they pushed it into the river.

When the new canoe didn't sink, the men felt a glimmer of hope. That is, until they tried to load their cargo.

One less canoe meant divvying up the cargo and

redistributing the weight across the remaining canoes. As a result, the six canoes were so weighed down that they were only a few inches from being completely submerged.

To help remedy the problem, the men cut some buriti-palm branches, bundled them together, and attached them to the sides of the canoes. The palm branches acted as buoys, helping to lift the heavy canoes up high enough to keep the water from rushing over the sides.

An hour and a half later, the expedition was once again heading down the River of Doubt. It wasn't long before the current picked up, and they were facing another series of rapids.

Everyone knew it was a risk to charge through the rapids. But it was also a risk to be overly cautious.

"On such a trip it is highly undesirable to take . . . risks, for the consequences of disaster are too serious; and yet if no risks are taken, the progress is so slow that disaster comes anyhow," Roosevelt stated.

With no time to waste, they threw caution aside. The *camaradas* steered the six canoes right into the wild waters.

"The two biggest rapids we only just made," Roosevelt wrote. "And after each we had hastily to push ashore in order to bail. In one set of big ripples or waves my canoe was nearly swamped."

The canoes managed to make it through unharmed, and the group's risky decision had paid off. This time.

CHAPTER 10

Risking It

March 15, 1914
Day 17

The next day the water was calm, and the expedition was making better time.

To speed things up even more, Rondon was using a different mapping method called the "moveable sighting" process. Although it was faster, the method was not as accurate and Rondon didn't like it. But he decided it was best to use this method, for now. It allowed Rondon and Lyra to take measurements based on sightings of Kermit's moving canoe.

Since they had been making such good time, the expedition set out early that morning. As the *camaradas* paddled down the smooth river, they could see the surrounding forest peppered with Brazil's famous rubber trees, which ranchers harvested for a milky-white sap called latex.

But within a short time, the surrounding landscape began to change from towering trees to rocky hills. Soon, they once again heard the sound of thundering rapids. Paddling the canoes around a curve, they saw an island in the middle of the white foaming water, splitting the river in half.

Kermit's canoe stopped on the left bank, just above the rapids, and waited for Rondon's canoe to catch up. When Rondon arrived, he ordered Kermit to wait there while he and Lyra scouted from the river's shoreline to determine if the rapids were passable or if a portage would need to be built.

While Rondon and Lyra checked out the area, Kermit decided to find out if it would be easier to travel down the other side of the river, hoping to save them some time. Kermit ordered João and Simplicio to paddle the canoe toward the island in the middle of the river, so they could get a better look at the right side of the river.

João and Simplicio didn't want to disobey Rondon's order to stay put, but they didn't want to disobey Kermit's order, either. Feeling obligated, they started paddling the canoe downstream toward the island. Once there, Kermit, the *camaradas*, and Kermit's dog, Trigueiro, climbed out of the canoe and investigated the other side of the river. It looked not only impossible to go down—even with empty canoes—but the shoreline's terrain looked too difficult to even build a portage.

After climbing back into the canoe, Kermit ordered João and Simplicio to return to the other side of the river. They began paddling the small canoe upstream, but before they had gotten very far, a shifting whirlpool spun the canoe around, pushing them toward the rapids and right in the path of a waterfall!

With the canoe turned sideways, waves and waves of water rushed in. Kermit shouted to João, the helmsman, to turn the front end of the canoe around. Using every ounce of strength, João was able to straighten it out. But it didn't stop them from heading nose first over the waterfall.

Roosevelt watched in terror as his son disappeared over the water's edge. He and Cherrie hurriedly climbed out of their own canoe and ran down along the bank of the river, making their way toward the waterfall.

At the bottom, Kermit's canoe was still upright but it was filled with water and close to sinking. João and Simplicio frantically worked their paddles, trying desperately to get the canoe to the bank.

They were nearly there when another shifting whirlpool ripped them away. The canoe was flung to the middle of the river, where it quickly filled up with water and capsized. Kermit, João, Simplicio, and Trigueiro the dog were dumped into the river along with ten days' worth of food rations and tools for boat building.

João grabbed a rope that was tied to the bow and pulled the canoe while trying to swim toward the shore. But the force of the current tore it from his hands.

Clutching his rifle, Kermit, along with his dog, climbed on top of the overturned canoe. Within seconds, they were swept down the rapids. The canoe rolled, throwing Kermit off, and the raging river carried him right over another waterfall. The water pounded Kermit's helmet down over his face and held him under the water's surface.

Fighting his way back up, Kermit gasped for breath. Now in swift—but somewhat calmer—water, Kermit willed himself to swim toward a branch hanging over the river. Knowing it was his best and, most likely, only chance to save himself, he reached up. His arm burned with fatigue as his wet hand seized the branch. With his last bit of strength, Kermit pulled himself out of the water and climbed onto the river's muddy edge. His dog, Trigueiro, climbed up onto the bank and sat next to him.

Shaken and dripping wet, they started walking back to the others. Trigueiro ran ahead while Kermit followed, keeping close to the bank. When Kermit was coming down a hill, he ran into Rondon and Lyra.

Although Rondon was relieved to see that Kermit was alive, he was also angry that the young man had disobeyed his order. Rondon kept his temper under control but made the chaffing remark, "Well, you have had a splendid bath, eh?"

Kermit explained what had happened and told them that he thought everyone was safe, believing that João and

Rondon was a great leader who commanded the respect of the expedition members.

Simplicio had also been able to swim to the bank. Kermit didn't know what happened to the canoe, telling them it had disappeared in the whirlpool.

While Kermit went back upstream, Rondon and Lyra decided to continue scouting the area downstream. They wanted to take a look at the second waterfall.

It wasn't long before Rondon and Lyra saw João walking toward them. When Rondon questioned him, João told a different version of events. João said that after Kermit looked over the rapids, he ordered them to go down them—even though João and Simplicio told him that they were impassable. In spite of their warning, Kermit repeated the order, and the two men felt obligated to obey.

What really happened, no one will ever know. João's version may have been true. Or he may have been afraid of the consequences for disobeying Rondon's order. At that moment, what they did know was that Simplicio was missing and so was the canoe with ten days' worth of food and tools.

No one searched harder for Simplicio than Kermit. He spent hours walking up and down the river, hoping to find him. But Simplicio's body was never found. The men speculated that when he went over the waterfall, his body must have been pulled underwater and beaten against the boulders, drowning him.

The canoe was also gone. It must have been smashed to pieces against the boulders and swept away, with no trace left of it.

Though the men knew that danger and death were real possibilities on the expedition, the pain from the loss of Simplicio was felt by everyone. A feeling of despair was also edging its way into the group.

"Misfortune still pursues us and this morning we lost another canoe and one of the boys was drowned. Today's misfortune is a tragedy!" Cherrie wrote in his diary.

The following morning, after everyone listened to Rondon's Order of the Day, a post and a marker were placed at their campsite. The sign read: "In these rapids died poor Simplicio."

CHAPTER 11

The Arrow

March 16, 1914

Day 18

After acknowledging Simplicio's death and naming the waterfall after him, the men once again began the backbreaking job of building another portage. Kermit continued his search for Simplicio's body. But all that he was able to find was an oar, a box of rations, and more rapids.

While the *camaradas* built the portage and Kermit looked for Simplicio, Rondon set off with his dog, Lobo, to hunt for game and Brazil nuts. Walking along the bank of the river, Rondon was about a mile away from their camp when he heard the sound of spider monkeys, the largest primate in the Amazon rain forest. They would make a good meal.

Rondon crouched down, taking cover in the thick vegetation, and quietly advanced toward the sound of the monkeys. While he kept his eyes focused on the trees above, trying to spot them, Lobo ran ahead.

More animals of the Amazon:

Top: A spider monkey has a prehensile tail but no

thumbs and spends most of its time in trees.

Bottom: A peccary can be ferocious when threatened and makes

a rattling sound by chattering its teeth to scare off predators.

Trying not to make a sound, Rondon listened for the monkeys. Instead, he heard Lobo cry out in agony.

Rondon immediately thought that a jaguar or the wild boar–like peccary was attacking his dog—until he heard a chorus of voices. He recognized it as the sound that some of the Indian tribes would make when they were ready to attack an enemy.

Lobo staggered back to Rondon, blood dripping from his body. Two arrows had pierced him. One had struck his stomach, just below his heart. The other had hit his right leg, and the muscle was ripped away.

Rondon fired his rifle into the air. He waited a few moments, hoping the sound would scare the Indians away. But the voices were coming closer.

He fired his gun again, but the Indians were still heading his way.

Rondon was torn. He wanted to help his dog, but he didn't want to fight the Indians. If Rondon wanted peace, he knew there was only one thing he could do.

Rondon left his dying dog and ran as fast as he could back to camp.

When he arrived, Rondon was greeted with more bad news. The canoe that had taken them four precious days to build had smashed on the rocks and sunk. They were now down to just four canoes for twenty-one men.

At that moment, Rondon was more concerned about the Indians and Lobo. He asked Kermit, Lyra, Dr. Cajazeira, and Antonio Pareci to go back with him. Before leaving, he quickly grabbed some tools and beads, which he planned to give to the Indians as a peace offering.

The group retraced Rondon's steps, and they soon found a trail of blood that led them to Lobo, who had tried to follow Rondon back to camp. They examined Lobo's dead body and found one of the arrowheads still inside the dog. When Rondon inspected it, he knew right away that it did not belong to the Nhambiquara. But he had no idea which tribe it came from.

The mysterious arrows belonged to the Cinta Larga Indians. Although the Cinta Larga were expert hunters and fishermen, skilled at surviving in the ruthless jungle, they were even more primitive than the Nhambiquara.

Unlike the Nhambiquara Indians, who had made the expedition's original dugout canoes, the Cinta Larga Indians had never even seen a boat until they saw the Roosevelt-Rondon Expedition go by. They also had never seen or used a fishing pole and hook to catch a fish. Instead, they made long wooden arrows without a blade on the tip to spear the fish. Or they used a poison that paralyzed the fish, making it easy to scoop them out of the water.

The impenetrable forest and rough river had kept the Cinta Larga so isolated that they had never seen a white man before, and they were shocked to see the men's beards. The men in the Cinta Larga tribe didn't have whiskers; their faces were naturally bare and hairless. So when they saw Kermit's and Cherrie's bearded faces, they wondered if they were even human or some kind of animal.

Since first spotting the expedition members, the Cinta Larga had been holding tribal meetings, trying to decide if they should go to war and kill the invaders. Since they weren't governed by a chief, the decision had to be unanimous.

If the Cinta Larga did attack and, ultimately, kill all the men on the expedition, there would be a big celebration. One of the highlights would involve cooking and eating their enemies' dead bodies. This was the only time cannibalism was allowed in the tribe.

Nevertheless, reaching a unanimous decision about going to war was proving difficult. Rondon, however, knew exactly how he was going to proceed.

Despite the fact that the Cinta Larga had attacked and killed his beloved dog, Rondon left the tribe some beads and metal axes in an effort to keep the peace. Even so, Rondon and the others knew that this gesture of goodwill was no guarantee that the Cinta Larga wouldn't attack.

At the end of the day, Cherrie expressed everyone's growing concerns in his diary:

"Misfortune still pursues us! From last night's camp we came only a few kilometers to another series of rapids . . . In addition to losing the canoe we have a very possible danger from the <u>Indians</u>! . . . Our position is really a very serious one. Provisions are every day decreasing. It is impossible to go back. The journey ahead is undoubtedly a <u>very long</u> one. The difficulties to overcome can only be judged by what we have passed through!"

CHAPTER 12

No Doubt

March 17, 1914
Day 19

There was no denying that their situation was looking grim. "So far the country had offered little in the way of food except palm-tops," Roosevelt wrote. "We had lost four canoes and one man. We were in the country of wild Indians, who shot well with their bows. It behooved us to go warily, but also to make all speed possible, if we were to avoid serious trouble."

With just four canoes left, there wasn't enough room to fit all of their equipment and supplies. This was a serious problem, but the expedition couldn't risk stopping and building new ones. They had to keep moving.

"It was not wise to spend the four days necessary to build new canoes where we were, in danger of attack from the Indians," Roosevelt wrote.

So everyone had to leave some of their belongings behind—tents, surveying instruments, and clothes. Roosevelt gave an extra pair of pants to Paixão Paishon, the *camarada* whose only pair had been torn to shreds when he had helped build the now-wrecked canoe. Since that time, Paishon had been wearing his underdrawers. With the loads lightened, the group was finally able to take off down the river. But like the cargo, not everyone could fit in the canoes, so thirteen of the men had to walk.

Armed with guns, Rondon, Lyra, Kermit, Cherrie, and nine of the *camaradas* were traveling in a single-file line, as close to the river's edge as possible. Three *camaradas* were assigned the difficult task of clearing the path of vines and dense foliage. The extra work made it impossible for them to keep up with the canoes.

On the river, the canoes were tied together in pairs to form a balsa, or raft. Roosevelt was in charge of one pair of canoes, and Dr. Cajazeira was in charge of the other. There were six *camaradas* traveling with Roosevelt since three of them were unable to walk. The insects had made a meal out of their feet, causing them to swell up painfully.

The canoes had traveled only three miles down the river when they were faced with rapids. Fortunately, they were able to unload the cargo, carry it, and run the canoes empty down the river without a problem. But ten minutes later, when Roosevelt's canoes came around a sharp turn, they were unexpectedly swept into another series of rapids.

Panicked, everyone tried to paddle and push the canoes away from the boulders. But the canoes were too big and clumsy. The water shoved them toward the boulders. Above the din of the rapids, the men could hear the wooden canoes scraping and thumping into the rocks. After mooring the canoes safely to the bank, the men began to unload the canoes for another long portage.

"We got through by the skin of our teeth . . . It was a narrow escape from a grave disaster," Roosevelt wrote.

While they were setting up camp at the foot of the rapids, Rondon and Kermit found a deep and narrow stream entering the River of Doubt. After Rondon measured its width and depth, he determined it was the largest tributary they had encountered so far.

"There was no longer any question that the Dúvida (River of Doubt) was a big river, a river of real importance . . . But we were still wholly in the dark as to where it came out," Roosevelt wrote.

The following morning, on March 18, Rondon spent extra time setting up a large post near the newly found tributary. Afterward, everyone gathered around it. Rondon read his Order of the Day, which was to officially name the tributary. An oval-shaped wooden sign was nailed to the post with the name "Rio Kermit" carved into it. He continued to tell them that the River of Doubt was now officially named the Rio Roosevelt.

From left to right: Cherrie, Lyra, Dr. Cajazeira, Roosevelt, Rondon, and Kermit stand near the post marking the newly named Rio Roosevelt.

When Rondon finished, he led everyone in giving three rounds of cheers in honor of the United States, Roosevelt, and Kermit. The *camaradas* "hip-hip-hurrahed" with enthusiasm. "I had urged, and Kermit had urged, as strongly as possible that the name be kept as Rio da Dúvida [River of Doubt]. We felt that the 'River of Doubt' was an unusually good name . . . But my kind friends insisted otherwise, and it would be churlish of me to object . . . I was much touched by their action, and the ceremony itself," Roosevelt wrote.

So Roosevelt responded by leading everyone in three cheers for Brazil, and then for Rondon, and Lyra, and the doctor, and finally the *camaradas*. After the shouts died down, Lyra called out that everyone had been cheered but Cherrie. So the group gave three wholehearted cheers for Cherrie, and everyone's spirits were lifted briefly.

After the ceremony, the canoes were heading back down the river while the rest of the men continued to walk along the river's edge. Everyone was feeling happy as they were making good time that day.

The men who were walking found themselves on an old Indian path, so they didn't have to spend valuable time and energy carving out a trail. But the threat of an attack weighed heavily on their minds.

Sometimes they could hear voices. But when the expedition looked around, they couldn't see anyone.

When the group suddenly came upon an Indian village, their minds were somewhat eased when they saw that it had just been abandoned. They figured the natives had fled to avoid a fight. But Rondon wasn't taking any chances. He left them gifts—an ax, a knife, and a string of red beads.

"There is no doubt that there are many Indians on all sides about us," Cherrie wrote. "If they are to prove friendly or hostile remains to be seen."

While the men walked, they were not only keeping an eye out for Indians but also for trees that would be suitable for making two new canoes. They had made a crucial mistake the last time. The wood from the tatajuba tree proved to be too hard and heavy, and its lack of buoyancy contributed to the canoe's demise.

"The wreck of the canoe . . . left us seriously embarrassed," said Rondon.

Several hours and one set of rapids later, they came upon an area dotted with araputanga trees. Rondon believed this wood would be perfect for making the new canoes. The araputanga tree is similar to red cedar and almost as light as cork, making it better suited for a light canoe.

Although there was still a threat of an Indian attack, Rondon believed this was their best chance to build two small canoes. As a precaution, he had guards posted throughout the night. Rondon also got up at 2 a.m. to make sure everyone was safe.

The next day, the *camaradas* began chopping down two trees. They had a bad start when the first tree fell, knocking down several smaller trees into Franca's kitchen area. But nothing was badly damaged, and the *camaradas* continued to work hard.

Two days later it looked like the canoes were nearly finished. But something else occurred to set them back once more.

"It was discovered today," Cherrie wrote in his diary on March 20, "that someone or one of the *camaradas* has been stealing our emergency rations! Fifteen of the boxes have disappeared!"

CHAPTER 13

True Colors

March 21, 1914
Day 23

In the wilderness, stealing food from other people is a major offense, especially when provisions are already scarce and the threat of dying from starvation is a real possibility.

"On such an expedition the theft of food comes next to murder as a crime, and should by rights be punished as such," Roosevelt wrote.

No one knew for sure who was stealing, but there was one person on the expedition who wasn't getting thinner. It was the same person they wouldn't assign the job of gathering palm tops because he would eat them all for himself. Their number one suspect was Julio.

They didn't have any proof or witnesses. All they knew for certain was that the deteriorating conditions had brought out the worst in Julio.

"There is a universal saying . . . when men are off in the wilds . . . they show themselves as they really are . . . A man may be a pleasant companion when you always meet him clad in dry clothes, and certain of substantial meals at regulated intervals, but the same cheery individual may seem a very different person when you are both on half rations, eaten cold, and have been drenched for three days—sleeping from utter exhaustion, cramped and wet," Kermit wrote.

For now, there was nothing the men could do but wait to see if more food disappeared and try to catch the thief in the act. In the meantime, Rondon placed guards near the food rations. He also told Paixão Paishon to keep a close watch of Julio.

On March 21, the day following the discovery of the theft, Roosevelt expected the new canoes to be launched and back on the river. When that didn't happen, Roosevelt became further alarmed when he learned that Rondon had not only told the *camaradas* to take their time working on the canoes but had also hidden this fact from him. Rondon had created the delay so he could use the time to explore and map another newly discovered tributary.

Rondon reported that, based on the new information he had collected, the River of Doubt wasn't as long as they originally guessed. Although everyone thought this was great news, Roosevelt knew this didn't change the fact that the food was still going to run out before they finished.

The next day, on March 22, the new canoes were finally launched. By 8:30 a.m., all six were back on the river. Even though they needed to make up time, Rondon began mapping the river again with the time-consuming fixed survey method since they now had more canoes.

The rapids were also slowing them down. The last set was so rough that it took six hours to empty the canoes, lug their cargo, and run the canoes down the river using ropes. They decided to camp at the foot of the rapids, and after the tents were pitched, Roosevelt called a meeting with Rondon.

The former president told Rondon that a detailed map was costing them too much time. He strongly urged their leader to abandon the fixed survey method once and for all. A less-detailed map would still be a valuable contribution, allowing other explorers to follow in their footsteps and fill in the details. Roosevelt firmly believed that it was in everyone's best interest to get down the river as quickly as possible, especially with the ongoing threat of hostile Indians.

Rondon disagreed. From his perspective and years of experience exploring the Amazon jungle, the low rations and hardships were typical. Starvation was something to be endured. He viewed the delays as an opportunity to spend time detailing the map. His priority was to get as many details for his map as possible, no matter what the cost. Besides, unlike the others, he believed that, overall, the expedition was going well.

"Were it not for the annoyance resulting from the delay, everything else was going favorably," said Rondon. "The

Food Rations per Person (measured in ounces)

FOOD	SUNDAY	MONDAY	TUESDAY
Rice	3.2 (about 24 spoonfuls when cooked)		3.2
Oatmeal		2.6 (about 2 small bowls when cooked)	
Bread (hardtack crackers)	20 (equals 20 crackers)	20	20
Tea biscuits	3.6 (about 17 cookies)		3.6
Gingersnaps		4.2 (about 16 cookies)	
Dehydrated potatoes	2.2	2.2	2.2
Dehydrated onions	1	1	1
Erbswurst (a sausage made of peas that turns into soup)		1.6	
Evaporated soups	1.2 (1 to 2 bowls when water is added)		1.2
Baked beans (canned)			
Condensed milk	3.4 (about 7 spoonfuls)	3.4	3.4
Bacon	8.8	8.8	8.8
Roast beef (canned)		11.3 (equivalent to a can of Spam®)	
Braised beef (canned)			11.2
Corned beef (canned)			
Ox tongue (canned)			
Curry and chicken (canned)			
Boned chicken (canned)	12.2		
Fruits: evaporated berries (jelly)		1	
Figs	4 (about 3 to 4 figs)		4
Dates			
Sugar	6.4	6.4	6.4
Coffee	2.1 (makes 5 to 6 cups)	2.1	2.1
Tea	1.1 (makes about 16 cups)	1.1	1.1
Salt	1.25 (5 ½ teaspoons)	1.25	1.25
Sweet chocolate			

This chart lists the rations that Roosevelt, Kermit, and Cherrie brought for their trip down the River of Doubt. They ended up stretching their daily ration to last a day and a half and gave over half of their daily bread portion to the camaradas.

WEDNESDAY	THURSDAY	FRIDAY	SATURDAY
		3.2	
	2.6		2.6
20	20	20	20
	3.6		
4.2		4.2	4.2
2.2	2.2	2.2	
1	1	1	
1.6		1.6	
			1.2
	5		5
3.4	3.4	3.4	3.4
8.8	8.8	8.8	8.8
			11.2
14			
	15.6		
		14.35	
1	1		1
		3.2 (about 14 small, pitted dates)	
6.4	6.4	6.4	6.4
2.1	2.1	2.1	2.1
1.1	1.1	1.1	1.1
1.25	1.25	1.25	1.25
3.2 (2 chocolate bars)			

sanitary condition of the expedition was good, and the quantity of provisions still existing was sufficient to assure us the termination of the voyage without scarcity of food." Rondon's view was in sharp contrast to Roosevelt's. Although Roosevelt could appreciate the importance of Rondon's work, lives were now at stake—which included his son's. He wasn't about to back down.

"Kermit was extraordinarily lucky to escape alive from the accident in which Simplicio perished," said Roosevelt. "I cannot accept seeing my son's life threatened every moment by the presence of Indians, more than that of any other member since his canoe goes at the head of the expedition."

Rondon knew that the Brazilian government had asked him to guide the ex-president of the United States and his men through the Amazon jungle to give them the best possible chance of making it out alive. So Rondon reluctantly agreed. But that didn't mean he had to like it.

CHAPTER 14

A Death Sentence

March 27, 1914
Day 29

For the past several days, it had been one series of treacherous rapids after another—about every fifteen minutes. That meant there had also been one long portage after another, eating up hours of their time.

"We are getting ahead very slowly," Cherrie wrote in his diary. "The frequent bad rapids making so many portages necessary. Our position every day grows more serious; the food supply less."

Despite catching two big piranhas that were divvied up with the previous night's dinner, along with two spoonfuls of wild honey and a handful of the ever-elusive Brazil nuts, the men woke up hungry.

Roosevelt had more than just hunger paining him. He was still attempting to fend off the flu-like symptoms of malaria that had been trying to overpower him since the first two canoes were smashed. Plus, he was suffering from dysentery, an infection of the intestines.

Cherrie, himself suffering from painful tick bites, was standing at the foot of the rapids and watched as three *camaradas* held on to a rope tied to two canoes that were careening down a narrow channel. When the canoes came around a sharp bend, jagged rocks unexpectedly grabbed a hold of one while a tangle of vines and fallen trees ensnared it. Before Cherrie could blink, the fierce current yanked the outer canoe loose and knocked it on its side. Within moments, the roaring rapids had sunk both canoes.

Refusing to let go of their ropes, the *camaradas* rushed into the river, fighting against the current. But instead of ripping the ropes out of their hands and smashing the canoes against the rocks, the force of the current kept the canoes pinned underwater.

Worried that it was just a matter of seconds before the canoes were swept away and wrecked, the *camaradas* screamed for help.

Cherrie ran toward them and charged into the river to lend a hand. But the force of the current was too strong. Knowing they needed more help, he ran down to the foot of the rapids.

"Two boats are capsized and held against the rocks by the current," Cherrie shouted. "If they wash loose, they will be crushed among the boulders!"

Everyone ran to help. True to form, Roosevelt was the first one in the river. Kermit and six of the men positioned themselves on a small island of rocks in a little waterfall right above the canoes. They dropped a rope down, and Roosevelt and the others, up to their armpits in water, tied it around the outermost canoe. Then they pushed and heaved while Kermit and the men above tried to pull the canoe free. For three hours the men labored anxiously in the water.

Finally, their hard work paid off: They were able to save the canoes.

But Cherrie noticed that Roosevelt was limping and bleeding. He had bashed his leg against the slippery, sharp rocks. Dr. Cajazeira carefully cleaned and dressed Roosevelt's bloody wound before the expedition got back in the canoes and headed down the river.

It was raining hard, making it difficult to see. Even so, within ten minutes, it was obvious that the rapids ahead were impassable. They would have to stop and set up camp in the rain.

Everything was drenched. But Franca, the cook, somehow managed to make a cup of coffee for them—despite the wet wood for a fire. Even so, the good cheer was short-lived when they went to sleep that night under soggy blankets.

The following morning, on March 28, the men moved their camp to the other side of the river, at the head of the

Roosevelt and Rondon pose for a photo in front of a waterfall they encountered during their trip.

rapids. Afterward, Rondon, Lyra, Kermit, and Antonio Correia scouted the area ahead to see how they could get the canoes down.

The men discovered that the foaming white-water rapids ran through a deep gorge between steep, rock-strewn mountain chains. They were discouraged even more after counting a total of six waterfalls. Rondon was at a loss. The terrain and river looked too fierce and treacherous to cross. Feeling despair, the scouting party didn't return to camp until midafternoon.

With one look at the expression on Rondon's face, the men braced themselves for bad news.

"We shall have to abandon our canoes and every man fight for himself through the forest," said Rondon.

"His report," Cherrie stated, "was practically a death sentence."

CHAPTER 15

Dire Straits

March 28, 1914
Day 30

Roosevelt didn't flinch when he heard Rondon's report. He knew it meant certain death for him—he was too sick and his leg was in too much pain to fend for himself in the jungle. But the former president didn't complain; he wasn't going to interfere if it was everyone else's best chance for survival.

Cherrie, however, did voice his concerns. He thought that abandoning their canoes and trekking through the jungle was a terrible idea. Even if they stopped to make new canoes, he didn't believe anyone would make it out alive. They were surrounded by Indians, and it would cost them too much in time and physical labor.

Kermit, too, was feeling panicked. His only concern was to get his ailing father out of the jungle alive. He was determined to do whatever it took to save his father's life, even if it meant risking, or even sacrificing, his own.

The young Roosevelt told Rondon that he had complete confidence in his own rope skills. Kermit believed that he would be able to transport some—if not all—of the empty canoes down the precarious rapids and waterfalls.

It was a dangerous, if not impossible, proposition. Nevertheless, Cherrie and Lyra backed him up, believing Kermit's plan was their best chance.

Rondon listened carefully and finally relented. But he knew it was going to be the toughest portage to date, and so he ordered everyone to leave behind what they didn't absolutely need.

"We thought we had reduced our baggage before," Roosevelt wrote. "But now we cut to the bone."

Roosevelt put on his spare pair of boots and handed his old ones over to his son, who gladly accepted them. Kermit's boots had been rotting off his feet from all the time he spent wading in the river trying to manhandle the canoes. The boots were just his size.

Although Cherrie was left with just the clothes on his back, he held on to his collection of bird specimens for the museum. He knew it was now impossible to add to the collection, since it would just add weight to their loads. Yet he couldn't help but notice four black vultures flying high above the forest.

Cherrie knew that this type of bird, a scavenging bird of prey, didn't live in the forest, so it was possible that once they traveled through this chain of mountains, they would reach open country, which would make their journey easier. Or so he hoped.

That night, Roosevelt's temperature rose. His leg was in worse pain, showing signs of infection, and the malaria was in full force. All through the night, Kermit and Cherrie took turns staying by Roosevelt's side, watching over him.

By daybreak, Roosevelt had only one thought on his mind. He loved his son, and Kermit had his whole life ahead of him and was engaged to be married. Roosevelt didn't want to take that away from him. And in his weakened condition, the former president believed he was a burden to the expedition.

Roosevelt called out to Kermit and Cherrie. When they reached his side, he said:

"Boys, I realize some of us are not going to finish this journey. I know that I am only a burden to the rest of you. Cherrie, I want you and Kermit to go on; I want you to get out—I will stop here."

CHAPTER 16

Do or Die

March 29, 1914
Day 31

Kermit and Cherrie refused to leave Roosevelt behind.

"There wasn't a moment from that time forward," Cherrie stated, "that either Kermit or myself didn't watch the Colonel [Roosevelt], to prevent him from carrying out what he felt was necessary . . . that he must relieve the party of what he considered a burden."

If Kermit was going to save his father's life, he knew what he had to do. From sunup to sundown, Kermit, along with Lyra and four *camaradas*, worked on getting the canoes down the six waterfalls. At times, the men were forced to cling to the steep, rocky mountainside with nothing to hold on to but narrow ledges, all while guiding the empty canoes down the rapids and waterfalls with long ropes.

After two days, Kermit and the men managed to maneuver three canoes down five of the waterfalls. But a fourth canoe smashed into some rocks and was destroyed.

"Men very disheartened," Kermit wrote in his journal. "Hard work; wet all day; half ration."

On the bright side, Rondon had managed to kill two barrigudo monkeys to supplement their meager dinner.

"The flesh gave each of us a few mouthfuls," Roosevelt wrote. "And how good those mouthfuls tasted!"

Their hunger made everyone start obsessing about food. A favorite topic of conversation was what they wanted to

Roosevelt (left) and Rondon pose with a bush deer they hunted during the overland journey. Large game was much harder to come by on the river, and finding food was a constant worry.

eat. Roosevelt craved a mutton chop with a tail to it; Kermit was hungry for strawberries and cream; and Cherrie couldn't stop thinking about pancakes smothered in maple syrup.

The lack of food was also taking a toll on their strength. Roosevelt was very concerned about the physical hardship the *camaradas* were forced to endure on so little food. Since he was sick and unable to help with the workload, he tried to give his food rations away.

"We had to watch him constantly," said Cherrie. "And [it] reached the point where if he didn't eat all of his share, either Kermit or I would take what was left and guard it until a later meal. We had so very little that every mouthful counted."

Even with all the watchful eyes on the food supplies, one person still wasn't deterred from stealing more than his share. One evening Paixão Paishon caught Julio red-handed stealing from the boxes of rations. That was all the proof Paishon needed, and he punched the thief in the mouth.

Julio ran to Roosevelt, crying. Roosevelt could see the fear and hatred on Julio's face as he complained bitterly about being mistreated. Although he got off easy—Julio was lucky they didn't kill him for the crime—his rage still simmered.

By March 31, Rondon and his men had transported all of the cargo to the bottom of the falls. Kermit, Lyra, and the *camaradas* had the remaining five canoes down to a point where they could be dragged over land.

That same day, Roosevelt and Cherrie, who was sick with indigestion, started the climb up and over the mountain, making their way to the new campsite at the foot of the rapids. But the pain was too much for Roosevelt.

Hunger, exhaustion, malaria, an infected leg, and now his heart were giving him trouble. Roosevelt threw himself onto the ground and begged Cherrie to go on without him—not once, not twice, but four times. Each time Cherrie adamantly refused to leave him. Cherrie not only respected Roosevelt as the former president of the United States, but he genuinely cared about him, like a brother.

Lying on the ground, Roosevelt tried to catch his breath. He didn't want to be a burden. If he was left to die, Kermit and the others had a better chance of surviving. But just as he was about to give up, a troubling thought invaded his mind.

"It came to me, and I saw that if I did end it [his life], that would only make it more sure that Kermit would not get out. For I knew he would not abandon me, but would insist on bringing my body out, too. That, of course, would have been impossible. I knew his determination. So there was only one thing for me to do," Roosevelt stated. "And that was to come out myself."

CHAPTER 17

Criminal

April 3, 1914

Day 36

A few days later, on the morning of April 3, the expedition found themselves just one hour away from their previous camp. The men had traveled only a mile and a half before the river's ferocity forced them to stop. Their slow progress down the River of Doubt continued to intensify everyone's growing anxiety.

"Instead of getting out of the hills at once, as we hoped to do, we are deeper among them!" Cherrie wrote in his diary. "The river's course is really a narrow rocky gorge where it runs like a mill race and wherever there is an obstacle of any kind the water becomes rough and dangerous . . . How much more of this we have no one knows."

A bright spot in their morning was eating turtle soup for breakfast. Kermit had found the turtle yesterday when he scouted the area. But, unfortunately, he had also discovered more rapids.

Their latest portage wasn't going well at all: One of the canoes had smashed into the boulders.

"A disaster, for we now have only four canoes!" Cherrie wrote.

Meanwhile, Rondon and a group of *camaradas* were clearing a trail over the hills and cliffs so they could drag the remaining canoes overland. The rest of the *camaradas* were busy carrying the cargo to the midpoint, which was the top of the first set of waterfalls. Paishon—who had continued to wear Roosevelt's spare pair of pants—was in charge of them.

Roosevelt, who was still weak and tired, was propped up against a tree. Cherrie—suffering from severe indigestion—and Kermit had helped Roosevelt walk to the spot where they were now keeping him company. While they sat reading, they occasionally glanced up to see the progress of Paishon and his group.

The men were nearly finished when Roosevelt happened to glance up and see Paishon set down a box. Wasting no time, Paishon turned around and headed back down the trail toward the camp to pick up another load. Roosevelt noticed that Paishon had left his rifle leaning up against the pile of boxes, but he didn't give it another thought.

Roosevelt focused his attention back to the book he was reading. Then he heard some muttering and groaning.

"One would know who that was by the groans," said Cherrie.

Roosevelt and Kermit laughed in agreement.

Julio was in a particularly foul mood this morning. A fellow *camarada*, Pedrinho Craveiro, who was assigned to guard the food and cargo at their last camp, had caught Julio stealing again. This time Julio had stolen some of their precious meat. Pedrinho and Julio had gotten into a fierce argument about it, and Pedrinho had told their supervisor, Paishon.

This time Paishon didn't punch Julio in the mouth. There was too much work that needed to be done by everyone, and he needed Julio to help. Instead, he gave Julio a stern warning.

Julio begrudgingly helped carry the cargo. But when Paishon reprimanded him for lagging behind, Julio became enraged.

After dropping his box, Julio, who was still muttering under his breath, picked up Paishon's rifle before heading back down the trail. Cherrie saw him take it, and he mentioned it to Roosevelt and Kermit.

They wondered aloud what type of animal had been spotted. Roosevelt suggested it was probably some monkeys or big birds, but either would be a welcome meal. A few moments later, they heard the gun blast.

"I wonder what he has shot at," Cherrie said.

Suddenly, the *camaradas* could be heard shouting: *"Julio mato Paishon!"*

"Julio has killed Paishon!"

Roosevelt jumped up and grabbed his gun.

"You boys guard the canoes and the food," he said to Kermit and Cherrie. "I'll go and warn the others."

Before Cherrie and Kermit could stop him, Roosevelt took off down the path, not thinking about his health. Dr. Cajazeira, who was nearby, followed him.

They quickly found Paishon. He was facedown, lying in a pool of blood. The doctor could see that Paishon had raised his right arm to defend himself when Julio shot him at point-blank range. The bullet had ripped through Paishon's heart, killing him instantly.

Roosevelt was now worried that Pedrinho—who was alone—would be Julio's next victim. Ignoring the pain in his leg, he forced himself to keep going.

As Roosevelt headed back to the camp, he turned his head from side to side, keeping a lookout for Julio, who might be hiding among the thick vines. When they finally reached the camp, the doctor walked in front of Roosevelt.

"My eyes are better than yours, Colonel," Dr. Cajazeira said quietly. "If he is in sight, I'll point him out to you, as you have the rifle."

But Julio was nowhere to be found.

It wasn't long before Rondon and Lyra arrived at the camp. "Julio has to be tracked, arrested, and killed," said Roosevelt.

Although Rondon and Lyra were both so angry they were ready to kill Julio, Rondon knew that legally he couldn't kill him.

"In Brazil, that is impossible," Rondon said. "When someone commits a crime, he is tried, not murdered." As a former deputy sheriff in the wild Badlands of the Dakota Territory, Roosevelt, however, believed that killing Julio was justified.

"He who kills must die," said Roosevelt. "That's the way it is in my country."

Despite what Roosevelt may have wanted, the responsibility of bringing justice for the crime fell on Rondon since he was the highest-ranking Brazilian military officer. Though Roosevelt was also a colonel and a former president, he was an American guest of the Brazilian government and could not risk going against his host country's laws.

To make Julio pay for his crime, the expedition would have to find him first. That would take time and resources—two things they couldn't afford. But if Julio still had the rifle, no one could stop him from killing again.

"We all felt that the cowardly assassin had run amuck and might be lurking in the thick forest waiting a chance to get another victim," Cherrie wrote.

When *camarada* Antonio Correia found the rifle not far from Paishon's body, Rondon decided not to go looking for Julio. The men speculated that when Julio ran away, the thick vines had snagged the rifle from his hands. After examining the beaten-down tracks through the forest, it appeared that Julio had turned around to come back for the gun, but, for whatever reason (likely fear), he had turned back around and went straight up over the hill.

For now, everyone was greatly relieved to find the murder weapon. Although they hadn't found Julio, and they were still worried that a killer was on the loose, they also knew that Julio most likely wouldn't survive on his own in the harsh and unforgiving jungle.

"It was questionable whether or not he would live to reach the Indian villages, which were probably his goal," Roosevelt wrote. "He was not a man to feel remorse . . . but surely that murderer was in a living hell, as with fever and famine leering at him from the shadows, he made his way through the empty desolation of the wilderness."

With the rifle now in hand, the men turned their attention to giving Paishon a proper burial. One of the *camaradas* had already respectfully placed a handkerchief over Paishon's face.

Though they didn't have any shovels, the *camaradas* used axes, knives, and their bare hands to dig a grave. They carefully lifted Paishon's body—Roosevelt and Rondon holding his head and shoulders—and lowered him into the shallow grave.

Out of respect, everyone removed their hats. After burying him, a cross was placed by his head. To honor Paishon, they gave a salute.

"We fired a volley for a brave and loyal soldier who had died doing his duty," Roosevelt wrote. "Then we left him forever, under the great trees beside the lonely river."

CHAPTER 18

A Turn for the Worse

April 4, 1914

Day 37

The following morning, Roosevelt woke up with a fever. He was weak and his infected leg was in excruciating pain from the stress and exertion he had endured the day before, hunting for Julio.

While Roosevelt tried to gather his strength, the men continued to haul the cargo and canoes. After Paishon's murder, Rondon had assigned armed guards to protect the men against a possible second attack by Julio.

Cherrie kept watch over Lyra and Kermit while they lowered the canoes down the rapids. With his rifle loaded, Cherrie made sure Julio wasn't on top of the cliff, ready to throw boulders down on them. Armed guards were also protecting the food and supplies as well as the canoes.

The *camaradas* made slow but steady progress. Roosevelt, however, took a turn for the worse.

Dr. Cajazeira, who had stayed behind to take care of him, noticed at 2:30 p.m. that the color suddenly drained from Roosevelt's face. His teeth started chattering so violently that the doctor couldn't get the thermometer into his mouth.

The doctor covered Roosevelt with a blanket and made him drink some quinine. An hour later, his fever went down.

After another hour, the canoes and cargo were ready to go. The *camaradas* helped Roosevelt get into the biggest canoe. He was lying down on top of the boxes, too sick to sit up. Soon it started raining; then came a hailstorm.

Roosevelt was wearing his rain poncho, and the doctor covered Roosevelt's face with his own felt hat. As the canoe made its way down the river, Roosevelt's temperature began to rise again.

Half an hour later, they paddled the canoes ashore to the right side of the river, away from the left side, where they believed Julio may have been hiding.

The rain beat down and the black river roared while Roosevelt shivered under the towering trees. It took time to set up the new camp, and by nightfall, Roosevelt's temperature was so high he was delirious.

He kept repeating, over and over again, the lines from Samuel Taylor Coleridge's famous poem "Kubla Khan":

" 'In Xanadu did Kubla Khan a stately pleasure dome decree
In Xanadu did Kubla Khan a stately pleasure dome decree
In Xanadu did Kubla Khan a stately pleasure dome
decree . . .' "

Kermit was feeling panicked. He sat by his father, watching over him.

When Roosevelt wasn't reciting the haunting poem, he talked randomly. He was worried about the decreasing food supply. Sometimes he was aware that Kermit was there by his side, and he would ask his son, "Did Cherrie have a good dinner tonight?"

"Yes, Father, Cherrie had a fine dinner," Kermit replied, trying to soothe his father's mind.

"That is good," Roosevelt said.

But other times Roosevelt wasn't aware that Kermit was there, and he would keep saying to himself, "I can't work now, so I don't need much food, but he [Kermit] and Cherrie have worked all day with the canoes, they must have part of mine."

Then Roosevelt would become aware of Kermit's presence and again ask, "Did Cherrie have a good dinner tonight?"

Cherrie, who was resting nearby in a hammock, could hear the conversation. He feared that Roosevelt wouldn't live through the night.

Roosevelt was so sick that he couldn't sit up. To protect him from the sun and rain, a tent was put up over his canoe.

At midnight, Dr. Cajazeira came to Roosevelt's bedside. He told Kermit to try to get some rest. In a last-ditch effort to save Roosevelt's life, the doctor filled his syringe with quinine and injected it directly into Roosevelt's abdomen.

At two o'clock in the morning, Roosevelt realized that even though he didn't want to die, he might not have a choice in the matter. He felt desperate to make it clear that if he fell into a coma or died, they were to leave him behind. So instead of calling out to Kermit, Roosevelt called out to Rondon.

Rondon quickly got out of his hammock and went over to Roosevelt. When Roosevelt looked at him, his stern expression startled Rondon.

"My dear Colonel Rondon," said Roosevelt. "This expedition must proceed without further delay. It must go on at once. Please give the order."

Rondon could see that Roosevelt was near death, and he tried to reassure him. At first, he told Roosevelt that he would give the order. But then Rondon tried to convince him otherwise.

"Colonel Roosevelt, this is your expedition," said Rondon. "If it went on, it would have to go without you, and therefore it couldn't be the Roosevelt expedition any longer. You see, you are the expedition. So the rest of us must wait for you."

Roosevelt looked unconvinced, but he was too sick to argue. A few hours later, when the sun began to rise, Roosevelt's fever slowly inched down.

Miraculously, he had lived through the night. A feeling of relief swept through the men, especially Kermit. But the nightmarish sight of his father near death and his feelings of helplessness were forever seared in Kermit's mind, haunting him.

Despite Roosevelt's improvement, Kermit knew that even though his father was no longer delirious, he was still weak and vulnerable to a relapse. It would be a long fight for everyone to make it out of the jungle alive.

CHAPTER 19

Left for Dead

April 5, 1914
Day 38

Roosevelt wasn't the only expedition member fighting malaria. Two of the *camaradas* were also so sick they couldn't work. And on the very morning that Roosevelt's temperature began to drop, Kermit's began to rise.

"I have fever but not very bad . . . much worried," Kermit wrote in his diary.

Ignoring his fever and still worried about his father, Kermit worked with the *camaradas* to get the canoes down the rapids. He also hiked for miles with Rondon and Lyra, scouting the area ahead to find out what they were up against.

The men brought back unexpected good news.

"R[ondon], L[yra], and I . . . found that after these rapids we're out of the hills," Kermit wrote.

Camarada Antonio Pareci also came running into camp with good news. There was a troupe of barrigudo monkeys nearby. Kermit, Lyra, and Cherrie grabbed their guns. The monkeys were moving with surprising speed through the tree branches. Even so, Kermit shot one and Cherrie killed two.

"They will give us a taste of fresh meat that we all crave," Cherrie wrote in his diary. "Our prospects look brighter this evening. The mountains, that have so long hemmed us in, seem to be falling away from the river. The river seems to be broadening."

Despite the flicker of hope that lifted their spirits, they were still worried that not everyone was going to make it out alive, especially Roosevelt. It was evident that he was reaching his limits.

Earlier in the day, the doctor and Rondon both agreed that their current camp was too muddy and uncomfortable for Roosevelt. So Rondon decided to move a half mile downriver. The doctor arranged for the *camaradas* to carry Roosevelt on his cot.

But Roosevelt flat-out refused. He wasn't going to be a burden. He would walk—if necessary on all fours—until he dropped.

"If I am to go, it's all right," Roosevelt had told the doctor. "You see that the others don't stop for me. I've the shortest span of life ahead of any in the party. If anyone is to die here, I must be the one. The others must look out for themselves. You are all strong and can make it."

With the support of Kermit, Cherrie, Rondon, and Dr. Cajazeira, Roosevelt slowly made the trek down and around the rapids to their next camp.

"From time to time, when he became very tired, he would rest either on his bed or chair," Dr. Cajazeira stated. "And so he bravely made the journey."

The following morning, on April 6, the four canoes were back on the river. With the loss of two canoes, some of the men were walking alongside the river on the right bank. Roosevelt was still too sick to walk and was again traveling in the largest canoe. Rondon and Lyra were traveling ahead of him and the others, continuing to map the River of Doubt. But their concentration was interrupted when someone shouted, "*Tenente!*"

Rondon and Lyra looked up from their work and scanned the area. They weren't sure who was shouting "Lieutenant" until they saw someone clinging to a tree branch that hung over the left bank of the river.

It was Julio. He begged them for mercy and pleaded with them to let him climb on board the canoe.

Rondon was stunned to see him. He thought Julio would have walked upriver, along its edge, to head back to where they had started the trip at the telegraph station. Instead, Julio had been following them.

"It isn't possible to stop the canoe now, and to interrupt

the survey," Rondon said. "Besides, it is best to wait for Mr. Roosevelt."

Without another word, Rondon's canoe passed him by. Desperate, Julio scanned the river, waiting anxiously. When Roosevelt's canoe was in sight, he shouted frantically for Roosevelt, telling him he wanted to surrender and climb on board the canoe.

Roosevelt didn't reply. He thought Julio was "craven at heart, a strange mixture of ferocity and cowardice." And the decision of what to do was clear-cut in Roosevelt's mind.

"I had no intention of taking a murderer aboard, to the jeopardy of the other members of the party," Roosevelt wrote. "Unless Colonel Rondon told me that it would have to be done in pursuance of his duty."

Without saying a word or giving a backward glance, Roosevelt gave Julio his answer. His canoe passed him by.

Julio watched as the expedition that he was once so eager to join headed down the River of Doubt without him, knowing he was left for dead.

CHAPTER 20

The Hunt

April 7, 1914
Day 40

The following morning, Rondon told Roosevelt that he wanted to send a search party back for Julio. This wasn't the first time Rondon had suggested it. He'd also mentioned it the day before after they had set up their campsite.

Roosevelt didn't like the idea then, and he still didn't like it this morning. A bitter argument between Roosevelt and Rondon ensued.

It would take all day to look for Julio, Roosevelt argued. They didn't have time to spare.

Rondon reasoned that with so many of the men sick, the time spent hunting for Julio would give them a chance to rest. But Roosevelt suspected that Rondon really wanted some time to survey a large tributary that flowed into the River of Doubt, which they had discovered the day before and had named Rio Capitão Cardoso in honor of Rondon's friend and colleague who had died while working in the Brazilian wilderness. Roosevelt remembered how Rondon had secretly delayed finishing the canoes in order to fill in the details of their map earlier in the journey.

Kermit didn't believe Rondon's intentions were pure, either.

"Rondon deliberately vacillated about Julio with 100 lies. He wants to wait and take the latitude but F[ather] won't let him . . . Rondon and Lyra begged to stop to send back for Julio whom 3 days ago they were in a blind rage to kill," Kermit wrote in his diary.

Cherrie echoed this feeling in his own diary:

"What was our astonishment to hear Col. Rondon announce that he intended remaining [sic] in this camp for the day!" Cherrie wrote. "And he intended to send a couple of men to look for the murderer Julio! To capture and carry him along with us to where he could deliver him to the military authorities! This resolution on Col. Rondon's part is almost inexplicable in the face of facts regarding our position."

The burden of feeding and guarding a prisoner was not something the expedition could afford to do.

"We do not know what difficulties are ahead of us or how long a time must pass before we reach a point where assistance can be obtained," Cherrie wrote. "From our point of view this delay and the trying to carry a prisoner places in jeopardy the lives of every member of our party. And the carrying of a prisoner passenger with us is a very serious undertaking."

Although Roosevelt strongly disagreed with the plan, he told Rondon it was his decision to make.

"Colonel Rondon was the superior officer of both the murderer and of all the other enlisted men and army officers on the expedition," Roosevelt wrote. "And in return was responsible for his actions to his own governmental superiors and to the laws of Brazil; and that in view of this responsibility he must act as his sense of duty bade him."

So Rondon sent two *camaradas*, Antonio Pareci and Luiz Correia, to look for Julio. In the meantime, he and Lyra surveyed the newly discovered river.

"To take the greatest advantage possible of the stoppage which had been imposed upon us," Rondon said, "Lieutenant Lyra and I occupied ourselves with the measurement of the rivers and the necessary astronomical observations for the calculation of the geographical coordinates of our position."

Though Roosevelt had conceded to Rondon's wish to stay, he pushed Rondon to send someone to scout the area ahead of them. At first Rondon resisted, figuring that they were out of the hills, so the chance of encountering impassable rapids was unlikely. But Roosevelt insisted, as they heard an ominous roar in the distance.

Reluctantly, Rondon ordered Antonio Correia to check out the area. The remaining *camaradas* who weren't sick were tasked with chopping down some trees to make spare paddles—also at Roosevelt's insistence.

Hours later, Antonio returned with bad news. There were more rapids and waterfalls down the river.

"It may well be that we are 'up against it' again and good and hard!" Cherrie wrote.

Despite this disappointing and worrisome news, Antonio also brought back something good—a pirarara, a type of catfish. It was three and a half feet long, which was enough to feed everyone. He handed it over to Franca to prepare.

When Franca cut the fish open and began cleaning it, he found the partially digested head and arm of a monkey!

"We Americans were astounded at the idea of a catfish making prey of a monkey," Roosevelt wrote.

Roosevelt supposed that the monkey must have been dangling from a tree branch, trying to take a drink of water from the river, when the catfish swam up and ate him.

The taste of fresh fish helped lift everyone's spirits. That evening, despite the persistent pain in his leg, Roosevelt enjoyed watching the sunset and the stars twinkling in the dark sky while waiting for Antonio Pareci and Luiz Correia to return.

When they finally arrived, Julio wasn't with them. They had spent hours shouting his name, firing their guns into the air, and even starting a fire, with the hope that the smoke would help Julio find his way back to them. But he was nowhere to be found.

It was possible that in a desperate attempt to survive, Julio had sought help from the Cinta Larga. If that was the case, he was as good as dead.

In the end, Julio's fate remained a mystery.

CHAPTER 21

Signs of Life

April 13, 1914
Day 46

The men didn't know how much more they could take. The rapids were unrelenting. They had been fighting them for the past six weeks, and the last six days had been no different. Barely ten minutes would go by before they were faced with another series of rapids, which meant another punishing portage.

"We were . . . on our way . . . but without much hope of getting far ahead. With what dread we watched each turn in the river to see what it held in store," Cherrie wrote.

On April 13, they nearly crashed another canoe when two paddles splintered against the rocks while battling the rapids. With no spare oars, they were forced to stop, chop down a tree, and make new ones. The process took three hours.

Meanwhile, Roosevelt was barely hanging on. At each portage, Kermit and Cherrie held him up as he walked. The bacterial infection in his leg was now so severe, he could barely hobble. A shiny, bright red rash, called St. Anthony's fire, covered his swollen leg, and pus-filled abscesses protruded beneath the skin. Just a mere touch to his leg caused unbearable pain.

The infection also left Roosevelt so weak that he couldn't sit up, forcing him once again to lie down on top of the boxes in the canoe in an uncomfortable position. Sometimes it rained so hard, he was drenched. Other times, the sun beat down, roasting him.

Roosevelt knew it was only a matter of time before the infection got the best of him. But he never complained, not even when Dr. Cajazeira cut open his leg, without pain-killers, and drained the abscesses.

"With it all he was invariably cheerful," Kermit wrote. "And in the blackest times ever ready with a joke . . . Father's courage was an inspiration never to be forgotten by any of us."

Despite how sick he was, Roosevelt always made a point of asking about the others on the expedition.

"Whenever one of the canoemen was ill the Colonel [Roosevelt] was the first to inquire about the man," said Cherrie.

Just about everyone on the expedition—with the exception of Rondon—had been sick. Even though Dr. Cajazeira administered daily doses of quinine to everyone, half of the *camaradas* were battling malaria. Kermit was still feeling ragged from it, but he was better compared to four days ago, when he could barely stand up.

Cherrie and Lyra had recovered from dysentery, but then Cherrie developed a cough and sore throat. It was difficult for all the men—even Rondon—not to feel depressed.

"This long series of rapids . . . has knocked a little of the cocksuredness out of Rondon . . . He has been discouraged and gloomy," Cherrie wrote in his diary.

But there was one glimmer of hope. When *camarada* Luiz Correia had taken a canoe out to fish, he had noticed an area where the vines had obviously been cut with an ax. Since the Cinta Larga didn't use metal tools, it could only mean one thing—they were near civilization! Still, that was three days ago, and they hadn't seen any signs since.

Now the only signs they had been seeing were more rapids. Until late in the afternoon, when it suddenly became quiet.

"At last!" Cherrie wrote. "After for more [sic] than a month's fighting rapids we are at a camp where their roar is not heard."

The following day, on April 14, they traveled twenty miles—much farther than their usual three miles.

Dinner that night was fairly good for a change, too. They ate fish, monkey, and a jacare-tinga bird, which is similar to a turkey. The *camaradas* also found a large pile of nuts that they gorged on.

Before the day was over, there was one more surprise

near the campsite: Kermit found a walking stick. The men speculated it must have belonged to one of the rubber gatherers who had been out exploring the area. They dared to hope that things were looking up.

But the next morning, on April 15, they were "a rather sorry crew." The nuts the *camaradas* had eaten were bad, and most of them were suffering from food poisoning—with vomiting, diarrhea, and dizziness.

Despite Kermit's painfully sore arms from the quinine injections, he took over paddling one of the canoes because most of the *camaradas* were too sick to work. His father was still deathly ill, lying down in the larger canoe that followed him.

For the next three hours, there wasn't a rapid in sight. Then, suddenly, Rondon began to wave excitedly. He was pointing and gesturing to the other canoes to paddle their boats to the shore. Rondon jumped out of his canoe and ran over to a wooden sign nailed to a post. The letters *J.A.* were burned onto it. They were the initials of a rubber gatherer, and it marked his territory.

Excitement swept through the men.

"It was the first definite mark that a civilized man had been on the river," Cherrie noted.

With renewed vigor, the men got back in their canoes. Less than an hour later, a house came into view. Cheers erupted.

The expedition paddled their canoes ashore. The men reached the house and realized it belonged to Joaquim Antonio—the man whose initials Rondon had found carved on a signpost.

Inside they found a large supply of food. As hungry as the men were, they didn't take anything. Instead, Rondon left a note and listed all of their names, letting the owner know they'd been there. Rondon was now confident that there would be other homes along the river where they would have a chance to buy food.

They returned to their canoes and headed down the river. Just a half hour later, Rondon spotted a man in a canoe. The man took one look at the motley crew and frantically paddled his canoe toward the shore, desperately trying to get away. He was convinced they were Indians and knew that no one who came down the river from that direction was friendly.

Rondon jumped up in his canoe and yanked his hat off his head. He waved it wildly in the air and shouted friendly assurances to the man.

Luckily, it worked. The man turned his canoe around and came right up to them. Rondon introduced himself, and the man told Rondon that his name was Raymundo José Marques.

Rondon informed him about their trip down the River

of Doubt, and when he introduced the man to Roosevelt, Marques was astonished.

"But is he really a president?" he asked Rondon.

Rondon explained that Roosevelt was not the president of the United States now, but he had been.

"Ah," said Marques. "He who has once been a king has always the right of majesty."

Although Roosevelt was too weak to sit up in his canoe, he appreciated the man's wit and courtesy.

Rondon continued talking to Marques and learned that he lived alone and could not spare any food. But the man assured Rondon that they would indeed find more houses down the river. He also gave Rondon a bamboo horn and told Rondon to sound it and fire three gunshots in the air so the people would know that they weren't Indians coming to raid their homes.

Rondon thanked him, and the expedition headed back down the river.

Although it would take two more weeks to complete their journey, from this point on, there would be houses along the river where the men could buy provisions with the money they'd brought with them on the expedition. They no longer had to fear starving to death.

"We had passed the period when there was a chance of peril, of disaster, to the whole expedition . . . We now no longer had to face continual anxiety, the need of constant economy with food, the duty of labor with no end in sight, and bitter uncertainty as to the future," Roosevelt wrote.

The families who lived along the river were an enormous help, selling the expedition two new canoes and setting them up with a knowledgeable guide. The group no longer had to worry what was around the next bend. Their new guide knew exactly where the rapids were, where to unload the canoes, and where the carry-trails were.

"Our adventures and our troubles were alike over . . . It was [now] all child's play compared to what we had gone through," Roosevelt wrote.

The men were overjoyed. Cherrie and Kermit celebrated by drinking the last few drops of whiskey they'd saved for just such an occasion.

On the evening of April 15, the rain finally stopped and the clouds parted. Looking up, Roosevelt and Cherrie saw the Big Dipper shining brightly in the clear, dark sky. Though the Big Dipper appeared "upside down" in this part of the world, it still felt like they were being greeted by an old friend from home—where they longed to be.

Roosevelt could at last take some comfort in knowing that their journey down the River of Doubt hadn't been for nothing. And he felt grateful to be a part of it.

"It was astonishing . . . to realize no geographer had any idea of its existence . . . For the first time, this great river . . .

was to be put on the map . . . rendered possible by seven weeks of hard and dangerous labor we had spent in going down an absolutely unknown river; through an absolutely unknown wilderness," Roosevelt wrote.

Mapping and exploring the River of Doubt had been a daring and deadly feat. The Roosevelt-Rondon Expedition had risked their lives to travel through a dangerous land— and in doing so, they forever changed the map of the world.

As Cherrie happily noted in his diary later that night, "Our work as explorers of an unknown river is of course finished!"

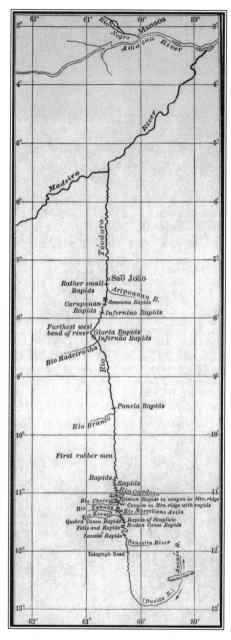

Roosevelt drew this map of the previously uncharted River of Doubt.

EPILOGUE

Six Weeks Later

May 26, 1914

Washington, D.C.

The tall arched windows were wide open, but it was still uncomfortably hot and stuffy in the Convention Hall's auditorium, located on the corner of L and 5th Streets in Washington, D.C. The eagerly waiting audience, overdressed in fancy gowns and suits, quickly realized it was no use trying to fan themselves to cool off. Flushed and sweating, they were also resigned to the fact that there was no escaping an odor of meat and vegetables, which was wafting through the windows from the market stalls outside.

Regardless, no one was going to give up his or her seat. Nearly five thousand people were packed into the auditorium to hear Theodore Roosevelt speak to the National Geographic Society about his trip down the River of Doubt.

There was a lot that Roosevelt wanted to say publicly for the first time. He wasn't going to focus on the zoological aspect of the trip. In fact, he wasn't even going to mention that during his time in South America, 2,500 species of birds and nearly five hundred mammals were collected for the American Museum of Natural History. Some of the specimens were new to science, and it was considered one of the most important collections given to the New York City museum.

Instead, Roosevelt wanted to talk about how the expedition had discovered and mapped a previously unknown river. Since the news was first reported, there were some geographers, including Sir Clements Markham, a British explorer and former president of the Royal Geographical Society, who had stirred up controversy by doubting Roosevelt's story.

"I feel somewhat incredulous as to Colonel Roosevelt having actually discovered a new river nearly one thousand miles long," Markham said. He even dared to suggest that Roosevelt may have mistakenly gone down a different river that was already known and mapped.

Roosevelt was both surprised and indignant. He knew the truth. The River of Doubt was an important discovery that changed the map of the world. And he could prove it, which is exactly what he planned to do tonight.

But first he had to get there. Roosevelt, who was accompanied by Cherrie, was running late. The National Geographic Society had scheduled a formal dinner in his honor before the lecture. Dressed in a tailcoat and white bow tie, he ate heartily and spoke at length with Robert Peary, the Arctic explorer who was credited with being the first to reach the North Pole.

Finally, at 8:30 p.m., Roosevelt arrived at the auditorium. At the first glimpse of him, everyone in the previously restless audience jumped out of their seats and clapped their hands, giving Roosevelt a thunderous standing ovation. Though everyone could see that the former president was noticeably thinner—he had lost fifty-five pounds on the expedition—they had no idea how momentous it was that Roosevelt was even alive.

With his stomach pleasantly full, Theodore Roosevelt walked onto the stage. His infected leg was getting better. When he had first arrived home by ship one week ago, he'd needed a cane to lean on.

The newspaper reporters who had greeted him as he walked off the ship were shocked at how thin and old he looked. They noted that his usually smiling face looked pained and pinched. But Roosevelt reassured them that he was feeling much better, especially since his recurring attacks of malaria had subsided, for now.

"I am still worth several dead men," Roosevelt jokingly told the reporters.

Despite lingering feelings of fatigue from the aftereffects of the infection and malaria, Roosevelt walked confidently onto the stage. When he started to talk, the former president was his usual exuberant self, gesturing wildly with his hands.

"I ask you to listen attentively to what I say we did," said Roosevelt.

Those in the back rows of the audience were having trouble hearing him, so they got out of their seats and rushed closer to the stage. Roosevelt looked over the map of South America that was set up as a visual aid.

"It is almost impossible for me to show you what I did on these maps because they are so preposterously wrong," he began.

Roosevelt turned toward a blackboard where he had sketched a map. With a piece of chalk, he drew in the River of Doubt, and said:

"I say 'we put it on the map' and I mean what I say. No map has ever yet shown the river . . . I can direct any man where to find this river . . . rivers stay put, so that the discovery we have made may be verified."

After Roosevelt clearly pointed to the exact location of the formerly unknown river, the audience listened in rapt attention to his stories of hardship and survival.

When Roosevelt told the audience that Rondon was hunting for monkeys so they could eat them for dinner, their jaws dropped open in shock.

"It will be perfectly safe to let me loose in the monkey

Roosevelt uses a map of South America during one of his presentations to show where the expedition traveled.

house of any zoo in the world," Roosevelt jokingly reassured them. "I have had enough to last me."

Although Roosevelt would never know that the Cinta Larga had been debating whether or not to attack and kill them—and had unanimously agreed to let the men live—he did mention that he believed the Cinta Larga were hostile only because they were afraid.

"But if a man shoots at you because he is afraid of you it is just as bad if he shoots at you because he hated you," Roosevelt said.

He also made a point in recognizing and praising Rondon and the work of his Telegraphic Commission. Roosevelt believed Rondon deserved worldwide recognition, just like the famous polar explorers Roald Amundsen and Robert Peary.

"I feel very grateful to him, to the Brazilian government, and to my Brazilian associates for having given me the chance to take part in exploring the upper course of and putting on the map an unknown river," Roosevelt said.

The adventurer spoke for nearly two hours. At the end, he asked the audience if there were any questions. No one said a word. After a brief moment of awed silence, Roosevelt exclaimed:

"I put a river on the map!"

No one doubted it.

*   *   *

Two weeks later, Roosevelt traveled to Spain to attend Kermit's wedding to Belle. He also made a stop in London to give a speech to the Royal Geographical Society—ending once and for all any doubt about the existence of the Rio Roosevelt.

In 1917, three years later, the American Geographical Society awarded Roosevelt a gold medal for "scientific achievement in the field of geography in the Southern Hemisphere." In his acceptance speech, he told them that the medal should really go to Rondon.

The following year, the American Geographical Society awarded Rondon the same medal. In 1956, the Brazilian government also honored Rondon by changing the name of the territory Guaporé to Rondônia, which is now a state—through which the Rio Roosevelt runs.

Although Roosevelt had survived his trip through the Amazon jungle, he would never fully recover his health. He continued to have recurring attacks of malaria and painful abscesses in his leg.

On January 6, 1919, nearly five years after his return from Brazil, Theodore Roosevelt died in his sleep. He was sixty years old. Many people believed that the hardships of the expedition had drastically shortened his life span.

But the adventure-seeking former president never regretted his trip down the River of Doubt. In a letter to a friend, Roosevelt wrote:

"I am an old man now, and I did have a murderous trip down South, but it was mighty interesting."

TEDDY'S TRAVEL TIPS*

When to Go

There is no perfect time to travel into the Amazon jungle. If the plan is to canoe down the River of Doubt, go when the river rises and flows continuously, which is during the rainy season (from approximately mid-December to mid-May). But expect to be uncomfortably damp and soggy most of the time.

How to Get There

Packtrains of mules and oxen are usually the mode of transportation used to reach the headwaters of the rivers in the Amazon. A sure-footed pack animal can carry cargo weighing from 160 to 180 pounds.

*Adapted from *Through the Brazilian Wilderness* by Theodore Roosevelt (New York: Charles Scribner's Sons, 1914, pages 353–369).

What to Pack

Survival tip #1: Do not overpack. A heavy load will slow you down. Each person should be limited to one waterproof duffel bag.

CLOTHING

* A sun helmet (to be worn in the open) and a slouch hat (to be worn in the forest).
* A khaki-colored shirt will do, but an even better option is a khaki jacket with lots of handy pockets.
* Long pants tend to bind at the knees while sitting in a canoe. A better option is a pair of loose-fitting knicker-bockers (paired with long socks), or shorts.
* Everyone has a differing opinion about socks, but thick wool socks will do a fine job.
* Gloves (to protect your hands from biting insects).
* Underwear. Always bring more than one spare pair of underwear (just in case).
* Sturdy, hobnailed boots made with good leather are recommended, especially for avoiding snake bites. Also pack a pair of moccasins with rubber soles.
* A durable rain poncho.

BEDDING

A hammock is the bed of choice in South America. Do not bring a camping cot. It will probably rust, and insects will crawl up its legs and make their way under the covers. A mosquito net is crucial if you want any shut-eye, and a light blanket will keep you comfortably warm, especially when you are wet and/or sick with fever and chills.

EQUIPMENT AND TOOLS

Survival tip #2: Along with a hunting rifle, always carry a small waterproof bag containing a compass, dry matches, salt, a fishing line, a hook, and a knife. These minimal supplies give you a fighting chance at survival if you find yourself lost and alone in the Amazon jungle.

* Lightweight freight canoes (wooden dugouts are not recommended) that are nineteen feet long and can carry one ton of cargo with ease. Pack six paddles in each canoe.
* Strong, high-quality pulleys and ropes to drag the canoes over long portages and guide them over danger-ous waterfalls.
* A lightweight waterproof tent that is long and wide enough for your hammock to swing back and forth between two trees.
* A mess kit (all-in-one plate, pan, and utensils).
* A machete to cut trails, and a rifle to hunt for food. A heavy rifle is not recommended for hunting jaguar and peccary, the only big game in Brazil.

MEDICAL KIT

Survival tip #3: Always take the necessary steps to avoid catching malaria. If you don't have any quinine pills, do not take a trip to the Amazon jungle. Also, bring large quantities of bug repellent.

Expect to get sick. Malaria, cholera, and dysentery are just a few possible ailments that will strike at any given time. Pack medicine accordingly.

FOOD, GLORIOUS FOOD

Survival tip #4: Since there is no guarantee that there will be nuts to gather, fish to fish, or animals to hunt, pack plenty of food rations to prevent starvation. This may seem like simple advice until you find yourself lugging a heavy load through the jungle. But remember: Never toss any food aside to lighten your load because when you're down to your last cracker, you'll wish you hadn't.

THEODORE ROOSEVELT—
CAREER HIGHLIGHTS

1882 First book published, entitled *The Naval War of 1812*. It became required reading at the United States Naval Academy in Annapolis. Roosevelt wrote forty-five books during his lifetime.

1882–84 Elected to the New York State Assembly. Fights corruption in state government.

1884–87 Rancher and deputy sheriff in the Badlands of the Dakota Territory.

1889–95 U.S. Civil Service Commissioner in Washington, D.C. Fights corruption and reforms the hiring system for federal civil service workers to a merit-based system. Roosevelt is considered the father of today's Federal Service.

1895–97 President of the board of New York City Police Commissioners. Cleans up police corruption and lays the foundation for the New York City Police Academy, one of the first in the country.

1897–98 Assistant secretary of the Navy. Orchestrated the beginning of the Spanish-American War.

1898 Lieutenant Colonel of the Rough Riders. Leads heroic charge in the Battle of San Juan Hill in Cuba. (Awarded Medal of Honor, posthumously, in 2001.)

1899–1900 Served as 33rd governor of New York. Improves working conditions for laborers. Preserves the Catskills.

March–September 1901 25th vice president of the United States.

September 14, 1901 Sworn in as president of the United States following the assassination of William McKinley.

September 14, 1901–March 4, 1909 26th president of the United States.

1902 Roosevelt the "trust-buster" fights corruption in the railroad, oil, and other industries with policies and reforms known as the Square Deal, meaning no crooked dealings. Under the Sherman Anti-Trust Act, he orders an antitrust suit to dissolve the

Northern Securities Company, the first of more than forty antitrust suits against big business monopolies during his term.

Settles Anthracite Coal Strike—first president to mediate a labor dispute. Working conditions and pay improve for coal miners.

1903–1904 "Big Stick Diplomacy." Treaty signed and construction of the Panama Canal begins (completed in 1914).

Adds Roosevelt Corollary to the Monroe Doctrine, stating it is the responsibility of the United States to intervene with force in South America in the event of instability.

1904 Roosevelt elected president of the United States for a second term—wins by a landslide. The election is noted for the largest popular majority vote ever recorded at the time.

1905 Negotiates successful Treaty of Portsmouth, ending the Russo-Japanese War.

Establishes National Forest Service.

1906 First American awarded the Nobel Peace Prize for his part in ending the Russo-Japanese War.

Signs the Antiquities Act—the first U.S. law to protect a cultural and natural resource. The first eighteen monuments included the Grand Canyon (later a national park), Muir Woods, and Mount Olympus.

Signs the Meat Inspection Act and the Pure Food and Drug Act, requiring the government to inspect and provide an honest statement of the ingredients on a label.

1908 Establishes the National Commission for the Conservation of Natural Resources.

1909 End of Roosevelt's presidency. Theodore Roosevelt was one of the most popular presidents to ever hold office.

Sources

Aberdeen Herald. "Col. Roosevelt's Story of His Last Great Adventure." June 5, 1914.

Boston Sunday Post. "Professor Cherrie, Naturalist of Roosevelt Expedition, Calls Wife Best Sportsman." October 11, 1914.

Bulletin of the Pan American Union. "Colonel Roosevelt in South America." Vol. XXXVII, July–December 1913.

Cherrie, George K. *Dark Trails: Adventures of a Naturalist.* New York: G. P. Putnam's Sons, 1930.

——. *Diary.* October 1913–May 1914.

——. "Theodore Roosevelt Memorial Meeting at The Explorers Club." March 1, 1919.

Diacon, Todd. *Stringing Together a Nation: Cândido Mariano da Silva Rondon and the Construction of a Modern Brazil, 1909–1930.* Durham, NC: Duke University Press, 2004.

Di Silvestro, Roger. "Teddy Roosevelt's Ride to Recovery." *Wild West,* October 2009.

Elliott, L. Elwyn. "The Rondon Mission." *The Pan-American Magazine,* August 1917.

Enciclopédia do Povos Indígenas no Brasil. "Cinta Larga." http://pib.socioambiental.org/en/povo/cinta-larga.

Harper, Frank. *Diary.* October 17, 1913–October 27, 1913.

Lewis, William Draper. *The Life of Theodore Roosevelt.* Philadelphia: The John C. Winston Company, 1919.

McCullough, David. *Mornings on Horseback*. New York: Simon & Schuster, 1981.

Millard, Candice. *The River of Doubt: Theodore Roosevelt's Darkest Journey*. New York: Anchor Books, 2005.

Miller, Leo. *In the Wilds of South America*. New York: Charles Scribner's Sons, 1918.

New York Times. "6,000 Storm Hall to Hear Roosevelt." December 11, 1914.

——. "Brazil Cordially Greets Roosevelt." October 22, 1913.

——. "Career of Theodore Roosevelt Was Part of His Country's History." January 7, 1919.

——. "Col. Roosevelt's Lecture." May 27, 1914.

——. "Kermit Roosevelt Goes West." September 2, 1908.

——. "Kermit Roosevelt, Hunter." August 2, 1908.

——. "Kermit Roosevelt Weds in Madrid." June 11, 1914.

——. "New Roosevelt Letter." January 30, 1922.

——. "President's Landau Struck by a Car." September 4, 1902.

——. "President Submits to Slight Operation." September 24, 1902.

——. "President Undergoes Another Operation." September 29, 1902.

——. "River of Doubt to Be Placed on Map." February 23, 1917.

——. "Roosevelt Kills More Game." July 8, 1909.

——. "Roosevelt Made Angry by Doubters." May 13, 1914.

——. "Roosevelt Now Homeward Bound." May 1, 1914.

——. "Roosevelt Returns 35 Pounds Lighter." May 20, 1914.

——. "Roosevelt Sticks to His Discovery." May 14, 1914.

——. "Roosevelt, the Boy, as Seen by Sister." February 16, 1920.

——. "Roosevelt Thought of Cuba When Shot." February 15, 1913.

The Ogden Standard-Examiner (Ogden, Utah). "Perilous Trip Is Described." January 17, 1928.

Omaha Daily Bee. "Colonel Put River on Map." May 28, 1914.

O'Reilly, Donald F. "Rondon: Biography of a Brazilian Republican Army Commander." Ph.D. dissertation. New York University, 1969.

Ornig, Joseph R. *My Last Chance to Be a Boy: Theodore Roosevelt's South American Expedition of 1913–1914.* Baton Rouge, LA: Louisiana State University Press, 1994.

Pringle, Henry F. and Katharine Pringle. "The House of the Happy President." *The Saturday Evening Post,* June 13, 1953.

Rondon, Cândido Mariano da Silva. *Lectures delivered on the 5th, 6th, and 7th of October 1915 at the Phenix Theatre of Rio de Janeiro on The Roosevelt-Rondon Scientific Expedition and The Telegraph Line Commission,* trans. R. G. Reidy and Ed. Murray. Rio de Janeiro: Typographia Leuzinger, 1916.

Roosevelt, Kermit. *Diary.* 1913–1914.

———. *The Happy Hunting-Grounds*. New York: Charles Scribner's Sons, 1920.

———. *The Long Trail*. New York: Metropolitan Publications, 1921.

Roosevelt, Theodore. *Diary*. 1878.

———. Letter from Theodore Roosevelt to Ethel (about Kermit while on Safari). June 24, 1909. Theodore Roosevelt Collection, Harvard College Library.

———. Letter from Theodore Roosevelt to Kermit (about Kermit's injuries). September 2, 1913. Theodore Roosevelt Collection, Harvard College Library.

———. *The Letters of Theodore Roosevelt*, ed. Elting E. Morison, John M. Blum, and John J. Buckley. 8 vols. Cambridge, MA: Harvard University Press, 1951–54.

———. "My Life as a Naturalist." *American Museum Journal*, May 1918. http://www.naturalhistorymag.com/picks -from-the-past/12449/my-life-as-a-naturalist.

———. *Theodore Roosevelt: An Autobiography*. New York: Charles Scribner's Sons, 1923.

———. *Theodore Roosevelt's Letters to His Children*, ed. Joseph Bucklin Bishop, New York: Charles Scribner's Sons, 1919.

———. *Through the Brazilian Wilderness*. New York: Charles Scribner's Sons, 1914.

The Seattle Star. "Bats That Suck Your Big Toe, Diamonds in

Rivers, Sweet Milk Trees—These Are Some Things Teddy Found in Jungles." May 16, 1914.

Smith, Francis Gow. "Brazil's Daniel Boone." *The Charleston Daily Mail*. May 12, 1929.

The South American. "Colonel Roosevelt's 'Rio da Duvida'" Vol. III, No. 4, July 1914.

The Sun. "T.R. Puts His River Duvida on the Map for Scientists." May 27, 1914.

The Syracuse Journal (Syracuse, Indiana). "Roosevelt Had Terrible Time." May 21, 1914.

The Washington Herald. "Roosevelt, Addressing 3,500 People, Tells of Putting River on Map." May 27, 1914.

Wynne, Arthur. "Steady Job Catching the Jabiru Bird." *The Fort Wayne News and Sentinel* (Fort Wayne, Indiana). April 19, 1919.

INDEX

Page numbers in boldface indicate illustrations or photographs.

ACKNOWLEDGMENTS

I want to give a big thank you to Marisa Polansky, Paige Hazzan, Jessica Regel, and Kelly Smith for their enthusiasm and encouragement. I also want to thank Ellen Duda for another eye-catching book cover.

Thank you to the staff of the Manuscript Division at the Library of Congress, who gave me access to Kermit's diary. To touch the actual diary that survived the trip down the River of Doubt a century later was truly a thrill in researching this story. A heartfelt thanks to my husband, Todd, who took photos of the delicate pages while I carefully turned them.

I am also grateful to Rodrigo Piquet, Chefia do Núcleo de Biblioteca e Arquivo do Museu do Índio in Brazil, for his assistance. *Muito obrigado!*

ABOUT THE AUTHOR

SAMANTHA SEIPLE is the author of *Ghosts in the Fog: The Untold Story of Alaska's World War II Invasion*; *Byrd & Igloo: A Polar Adventure*; and *Lincoln's Spymaster: Allan Pinkerton, America's First Private Eye*. She has worked as a competitive intelligence specialist for a Fortune 500 company, as a librarian, and as a production and copy editor. Her education includes degrees in English, journalism, and library and information science. She lives in Asheville, North Carolina.